ISSUES IN PROCESS MODELING: IDEF, UML & EPC MODELS

Vasileios Gougas

Vasileios Gougas
ISSUES IN PROCESS MODELING: IDEF, UML & EPC MODELS

ISBN UK: 9781912935970

Cover: Design by AKAKIA Publications

London, July 2022
Printed by European Printers
Published by AKAKIA Publications

akakia

46 Warberry Road,
N22 7TQ, London, UK
T. 0044 208 2457 849
publications@akakia.net
www.akakia.net

" To my lovely daughter Ioanna Maria"

"The hardest single part of building a software system is deciding precisely what to build. No other part of the conceptual work is as difficult as establishing the detailed technical requirements...No other part of the work so cripples the resulting system if done wrong. No other part is as difficult to rectify later."

Brooks, 1987

About the Author

Vasileios Gougas graduated from the Department of Electrical Engineering and Computer Technology, University of Patras, in October 2000 and received his second Msc in Telematics Management four years later from Danube University of Krems, Austria. He has also received another two Master Diplomas from Hellenic Open University in the area of Project Management and in the area of Adult Education.

He worked as a research fellow at the Technological Intsitute of Patras (TEI Patras) and at the Technological Institute of Larisa (TEI Larisas). He has published number of research articles in international journals and conferences. Today he serves as a teacher in the First Second Chance School of Trikala

TABLE OF CONTENTS

CHAPTER FOUR

CHAPTER FIVE

1

BUSINESS PROCESS

1.1 INTRODUCTION

In the Middle Ages, monks sat at tables carefully copying the scriptures. The father superior would make the assignments, perhaps giving the illuminated first page of a section to the most skilled artist, perhaps assigning the proofreading tasks to the elderly scholar with trembling hands.

Little has changed in centuries—supervisors assign work, perhaps based on training, skills, and experience, to various resources. At first the resources were only people, eventually supported by tools such as typewriters, printed forms, and adding machines. Eventually some of the steps were automated—the invoices were automatically totaled and printed, but only after people sorted the punched cards, or entered the data. Even though the performance of the work was at least partially automated, the management of the work had changed little—supervisors assigned work and monitored performance. Clerks passed the work from station to station. Lists were made to track the work—to find it when it went astray, and to measure the productivity. And an army of expediters searched for the problems and errors in the routing, and kept it moving.

In the last 15 years or so we finally have developed tools to not only do the work, but to manage the work that is made. *The process, know is managed by a computer program that assigns the work, passes it on, and tracks its progress*. Today many organizations are doing rapid and fundamental changes. Organizational computing systems are increasingly called upon to play a critical part in those changes.

New technical systems are no longer merely used to automate conventional work activities, but are fundamentally changing the way people work. Understanding how people work in an organization and redesigning their work configurations to make innovative uses of information technology to bring about superior performance is becoming an important prerequisite step to technical system development.

1.2 BUSINESS PROCESS

Most people associate business processes with the typical operations in a bank or claims processing in an insurance company. Such operations have led us to understand business processes as a sequence of activities, performed by various persons, the visible result being various pieces of paper, while these activities are being repeated following the same well-defined pattern.

We can give many definitions to the question what is a Business Process. First of all we can say that a business process is a set of activities that are executed in order to achieve a business objective. This objective is usually to offer the right product or service to a customer with a high degree of performance measured against cost, longevity, service and quality [JEJ 95]. For a complete description of a business process, aside the information describing constituent business process activities, we need information related to resources assigned to activities, i.e. objects necessary for the execution of the activities, like actors, documents, data and so on, control of the business process which describes 'when' and 'which' activity will be executed, the flow of data in the process and the organizational structure which consists of organizational units, people, roles, competence and so on [ATJU 95].

Process is a way for an enterprise to organize work and resources (people, equipment, information) to accomplish its aims and goals. Nowadays organizations try to organize work and resources to achieve a specific result for a specific customer. So we can have the definition:

"Business Process is a collection of interrelated work tasks, initiated in response to an event, that achieves a specific result for the customer of the process" [SMcD 01]. The phrase "... that achieves a specific result ...", means that the only reason that a process exists, is to deliver a specific result, which might be goods (e.g. products requested on an order) or services (e.g. information in response to a query).

The phrase "... for the customer of the process ...", means that the customer is the recipient of the result produced by the business process. In that point we must mention that the customer could be a person (external or internal to the organization (e.g. an employee)) or another organization.

Further more, the phrase "... initiated in response to a specific event ...", means that the process is inactive until it is triggered by an event.

The phrase " ... work tasks ...", means that the process is a collection of activities, steps, actions, tasks, made by a single or multiple actors. An actor could be a person or organization; generally we could say that actor is anything that plays a specific role to the whole procedure.

Finally the phrase "... a collection of interrelated ...", means that in a process, the steps are interrelated through sequence and flow – in simple terms the completion of one step flows into the initiation of the next step [SMcD 01].

Business Process Reengineering (BPR) is the activity of capturing business processes starting from a blank sheet of paper, a blank computerized model, document or repository. Once an organization captures its business in terms of business processes it can measure each process to improve it or adapt it to changing requirements. Continuous (business) Process Improvement (CPI) involves explicit measurements, reconsideration and redesign of the business process. Reasons citied for business process redesign include increasing customer satisfaction, quality of products, improving efficiency of business operations, reducing cost and meeting new business challenges and opportunities by changing existing services or introducing new ones [DGAT 98].

In many organizations the term workflow is used to refer to a specific category of automated business processes. The main characteristics of such processes is that they are specified and implemented in two tiers. The top tier consists of a single process, which we refer to as the workflow process, and it is implemented by a corresponding workflow application. The workflow application automates the coordination, control and communication of the basic process activities. These activities and the information systems or humans that perform them comprise the lower tier. During the workflow process enactment information or tasks are passed from the one participant (human or system) to another, according to a set of procedural rules that implement and automate the business rules defined by the workflow process [DGAT 98].

Currently, commercial available products support business process management and can be characterized as Workflow Management Systems (WFMSs) and Business Process Management Tools (BPMTs). Both WFMSs and BPMTs support business process definition or specification. However, BPMTs provide process understanding and analysis that can lead to process improvement, while WFMSs support process automation.

1.3 CHARACTERIZING BUSINESS PROCESS

Processes are distinguished into four kinds [McC92]:

- Ad hoc process,

- Administrative process,
- Collaborative process,
- Production process.

The basic dimensions along which these kinds of processes are characterized include [DGAT 98]:

- Repetitiveness and Predictability of the process and its activities,
- Mission criticality and value for the organization.

Ad hoc and Collaborative processes have no set pattern for coordinating activities and for moving information among process participants [Kor 94]. They typically involve small teams of professional performing both synchronous and asynchronous activities. Examples include many office processes such as business tax returns, product documentation and sales proposals. In such processes the ordering of activities is controlled and coordinated by humans. The basic difference between Ad hoc and Collaborative process is their relative value for the organization that uses them. In particular collaborative processes are very critical and they have a high value for the organization, while ad hoc processes are generally not critical since repeating the process can produce the desired result.

Administrative and production processes are repetitive and predictable. Administrative processes (such as routing an report) are not generally critical. On the other hand production processes are mission critical and so they have a high business value. A typical example of production process is loan application processing. The characterization of business processes is depicted in the following figure.

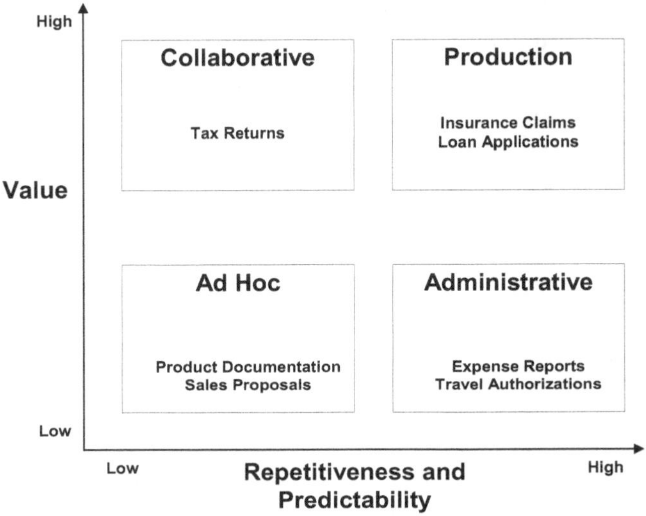

Figure 1.1: Characterization of Processes

1.4 WHY WE USE PROCESS MODELS

A single process could be quite involved. It can consist of many actors (people, systems, organizations) performing many tasks. In order to accomplish the overall task the actors must complete specified sub-tasks in a coordinated manner. Sometimes these sub-tasks can be performed in parallel some other times they are sequential. Some processes require repetition of sub-tasks. Most processes have decision points where process flow can branch depending on either the condition of the system or the particular process execution. In cooperative processes actors must pass information that may be the trigger for an actor to begin a sub-task. Other triggers are possible. Some processes are ad-hoc that is the sub-tasks do not have well-defined triggers.

Actors may not need to complete the entire subtask before they or another actor start work on another dependent subtask. Finally a process can look differently when described from the point view of different actors. A business process modeling methodology needs to be able to represent these different aspects of a process description. A good methodology will present the representation in a manner that is easily transferred into the tacit knowledge of the viewer.

In many fields of science, a situation or a system is not studied directly but indirectly through a model of the situation or the system. An aircraft mock-up used for wind tunnel testing like an architect's model of a building, is an iconic model – it resembles the physical object it represents, except that it is smaller and simplified.

Many definitions have been given about what a model is. Beer defines a model as "a representation of something else, designed for a special purpose". According to Wilson a model "is the explicit interpretation of one's understanding of a situation, or merely of one's ideas about a situation. It can be expressed in mathematics, symbols, or words, but it is essentially a description of entities, processes or attributes and the relations between them. It may be prescriptive or illustrative, but above all, it must be useful". A model is useful when it facilitates the description and the understanding of a complex situation.

There are various reasons why we use models. We model an existing system in order to understand and study it without preventing its operation. Models are also used to examine a risky situation is to be examined something that cannot happen in real. Finally, a model could be used to describe and analyse a future system before its implementation.

In business field, business process modelling refers to a collection of techniques that are used to model the behaviour of business systems, which is expressed in terms of processes. Managers and system analysts use business models in order to deal with the complex and dynamic nature of modern organisations. Models are used throughout the lifecycle of a process, supporting its definition, (re)design, implementation and continuous improvement. Therefore, modelling a business process should be considered as a continuous, endless activity similar to monitoring it, rather than an activity with a predefined end point.

Although the development and maintenance of business process' models is a difficult, time consuming, and costly project, there are very important reasons justifying the necessity of a modelling process, and great benefits to be obtained through it. The most important of them are following presented:

- A well-defined model facilitates understanding of the process by every process's participant.
- When a process model permits the decomposition of a complex business process at different level of detail, it enables focusing in the required level of interest, excluding details of lower levels.
- A model can show where processes cross organisation's boundaries, extend outside organisation, and participate in product distribution or in providing services to customers.
- Given the right notation, a model can be used to simulate the process in order to analyse it and to examine "what-if" scenarios.
- Models with formal syntax and well-defined semantics can be used to support process enactment.

Furthermore, there are some more potential uses of process models []Bro 02], [TDJM 03]]:

- Program Planning.
- Baseline for continuous improvement.
- Knowledge retention and learning.
- Process visualization.
- Training.
- Framework for metrics.
- Compliance, audit and assessments.
- Program execution.

Existing process modelling approaches mainly originate from the software engineering field. Several classifications for process models have already been suggested in modelling bibliography. In following we mention the categories of process models that will be represented analytically in the next chapters:

- ➢ The Activity oriented models that describe a process as a set of ordered activities, such as:
- IDEF0 and IDEF3,
- Swimlane Diagrams - UML Activity Diagrams,
- EPC (Event-Driven Process Chain) Model.

1.5 MODELLING CRITERIA

Using or not a model is not as important as the way that it is used. The kind of model that will be used in order to describe the business process is also important. The decision depends on the kind of process that is under study as well as the phase of the process that the model will support.

A business process is a set of internal *activities* which are the basic business process building elements and are executed in order to achieve a business objective which is usually to offer the right product or service to a customer with a high degree of performance measured against cost, longevity, and service. According to [ATJU 95] a business process model should encapsulate information related to:

(a) *Activities*,
(b) *Resources* assigned to activities, i.e. objects necessary for the execution of activities, like actors, documents, data and so on,
(c) *Control* of a business process which describes 'when' and 'which' activity will be executed,
(d) the *flow* of data in the process and
(e) the *organizational structure* which consists of organizational units, people, roles, competence and so on.

The applicability of a model is evaluated against the following criteria:

- *Ease of use* - how easily a modeller can learn to use the model and how easily a process can be modelled,
- *Comprehensibility* - whether the model enhances process understanding by the process participants, as well as whether it enables the communication between them,
- *Originality* - whether the model was developed for business process modelling or not,
- *Formal syntax and semantics*- whether the model has a formal syntax and well defined semantics,
- *Expressiveness* - whether the model can represent the relationships between the activities of the process and efficiently express issues such as iteration, time relationships, path selection, conditions e.t.c.,
- *Hierarchical decomposition* - whether the model enables the decomposition of process models and the construction of model hierarchies,
- *Analytical capabilities* - whether the model can be used to analyse the process and what kind of analysis it supports.

Moreover, there is a set of seven criteria for evaluating process modelling techniques [TDJM 03]:

- It must be able to model all the complexities of business processes listed above, to include:

    - Sequencing
    - Branching
    - Looping

  - Concurrency Constructs – fork and synchronize
  - Timeouts
  - Deadlines
  - Faults
  - Aggregation

- It must have a means of distinguishing roles and assigning them the various tasks.

- There must be an unambiguous graphical representation of the language.

- It must have a transaction model that allows for the description of how a process can be undone.

- It must specify how process instances will be triggered and identified throughout their execution

- It must have a means of specifying the characteristics of the business process that would be of interest to external users. This would include things like quality of service and pricing.

- The language should not mix in details of communications protocols.

1.6 PROCESS MODELS AND TOOLS

A business process model is a process abstraction that depends on the intended use of the model. When a process model is intended for business process analysis, improvement and reengineering it will be called business process model. When a model is intended for business process implementation and automation, it will be called workflow model. The main phases of a process are: Modelling, Analysis, Redesign (Figure

1.2). These phases are supported by two kinds of tools – as mentioned earlier – the Business Process Modelling Tools and the Workflow Management Systems [Tsa 99].

- BPMTs aim at the development of business process models for management, documentation or reengineering purposes. They focus on capturing and modelling details that are essential for business process analysis and simulation,
- WFMSs aim at the development and subsequent automation of workflow models and thus they differ in the level of detail their scope is located. Mainly they aim at transferring the process models in real world settings.

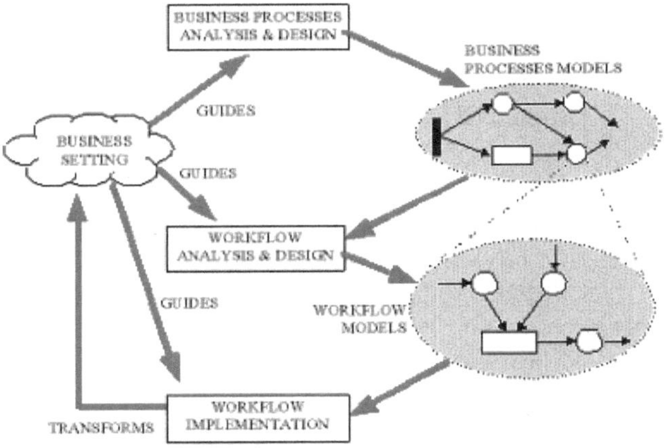

Figure 1.2: Business Process Lifecycle

1.7 METHODOLOGY FOR STUDYING PROCESSES

The world of business processes is very complicated, filled with politics, sensitivities, conflicting goals, so we must be very careful when we want to describe or represent a business process. According to [SMcD 01] there be four phases in order to approach the business process environment:

- Frame the process,
- Understand the current (as-is) process,
- Design the new (to-be) process,
- Develop use case scenarios.

According to Sharp and McDermott, the most important phase is the starting one that is to frame the process. Indeed it is a very critical phase as it prevents many common problems later. In this case we identify the set of related processes including the target process to be improved, by developing the overall process map. Then the process's boundaries must be identified, the process name, the initiating event, the customer and the result, the actors. After that the initial process assessment must be performed in order to consider, if necessary, and other participants that play regulative role in the process.

When the first phase is completed, second phase takes action. The "as-is" process must be understood. In that phase, process-modelling techniques make like. The current process must be modelled by the use of the different process modelling techniques that will be discussed in the following chapters. The process models gives critical information such as where the under study process is week and needs to be improved.

Then, the design of the "to-be" process takes place. In this phase the improvements or design characteristics are determined in order to achieve the process goals. When the characteristics of the "to-be" process are identified, the designing of the new "to-be" process begins, using of course the modelling techniques. Recent experience shows that when these implementations in the business process orientation don't take place, the result is often disastrous.

2

IDEF0 AND IDEF3 MODELS

2.1 INTRODUCTION TO IDEF0

Because organizations are very complex artifacts, it has been claimed that carefully developed models are necessary for describing, analyzing and/or enacting the underlying business process. A business process model is usually expressed by means of a graphical notation that must be able to capture all that relevant information from the model and additionally must facilitate the analysis of the modeled process by static verification and/or dynamic simulation [CBMBCF 02].

The IDEF0 Function model is designed to model the decisions, actions, activities of an organization or a system. It was derived from SADT (Structured Analysis and Design Technique) which was developed by SoftTech Corporation in the 1970's. The Air Force commissioned SADT developers to develop a function modeling method for analyzing and communicating the functional perspective of a system. The IDEF0's perspective is to efficiently describe complex business processes and systems as well as to promote effective communication between the modelers and the process participants.

IDEF0 is a modeling technique based on combined graphics and text that are presented in an organized and systematic way to gain understanding, support analysis, provide logic for potential changes, specify requirements, or support systems level design and integration activities. An IDEF0 model is composed of hierarchical series of diagrams that gradually display increasing levels of detail describing functions and their interfaces within the context of a system. There are three types of diagrams: graphic, text, and glossary. The graphic diagrams define functions and functional relationships via box and arrow syntax and semantics. The text and glossary diagrams provide additional information in support of graphic diagrams.

IDEF0 is an engineering technique for performing and managing needs analysis, benefits analysis, requirements definition, functional analysis, systems design, maintenance, and baselines for continuous improvement. IDEF0 models provide a "blueprint" of functions and their interfaces that must be captured and understood in order to make systems engineering decisions that are logical, affordable, and achievable. The IDEF0 model reflects how system functions interrelate and operate just as the "blueprint" of a product reflects how the different pieces of a product fit together. When used in a systematic way, IDEF0 provides a systems engineering approach to:

1. Performing systems analysis and design at all levels, for systems composed of people, machines, materials, computers and information of all varieties - the entire enterprise, a system, or a subject area.
2. Producing reference documentation concurrent with development to serve as a basis for integrating new systems or improving existing systems.
3. Communicating among analysts, designers, users, and managers.
4. Allowing coalition team consensus to be achieved by shared understanding.
5. Managing large and complex projects using qualitative measures of progress.

6. Providing reference architecture for enterprise analysis, information engineering and resource management.

2.2 SYNTAX

The structural components and features of a language and the rules that define relationships among them are referred to as the language's syntax. The components of the IDEF0 syntax are boxes and arrows, rules, and diagrams. Boxes represent functions, defined as activities, processes or transformations. Arrows represent data or objects related to functions. Rules define how the components are used, and the diagrams provide a format for depicting models both verbally and graphically. The format also provides the basis for model configuration management.

2.2.1 Boxes

A box provides a description of what happens in a designated function. Represent functions that show what must be accomplished. A typical box is shown in Figure 2.1. Each box shall have a name and number inside the box boundaries. The name shall be an active verb or verb phrase that describes the function, such as process parts, develop detail design, design system, e.t.c. Each box on the diagram shall contain a box number inside the lower right corner. Box numbers are used to identify the subject box in the associated text.

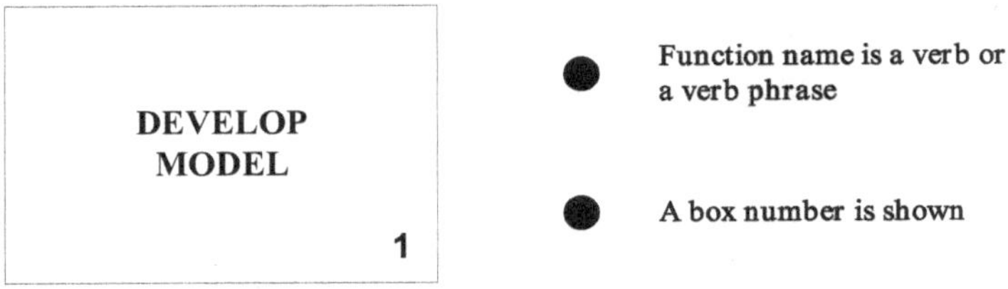

Figure 2.1: Box Syntax

2.2.2 Arrows

An arrow is composed of one or more line segments, with a terminal arrowhead at one end. Arrow segments may be straight or curved (with a 90arc connecting horizontal and vertical parts), and may have branching (forking or joining) configurations. Arrows do not represent flow or sequence as in the traditional process flow model. Arrows convey data or objects related to functions to be performed. Each arrow shall be labeled with a noun or noun phrase such as, specifications, requirements, and detail design, e.t.c. The functions receiving data or objects are constrained by the data or objects made available.

2.2.3 Box and Arrow Semantics

Each side of the function box has a standard meaning in terms of box/arrow relationships. The side of the box with which an arrow interfaces reflects the arrow's role. Arrows entering the left side of the box are inputs. Inputs are transformed or consumed by the function to produce outputs. Arrows entering the box on the top are controls. Controls specify the conditions required for the function to produce correct outputs. Arrows leaving a box on the right side are outputs. Outputs are the data or objects produced by the function.

Arrows connected to the bottom side of the box represent mechanisms. Upward pointing arrows identify some of the means that support the execution of the function. Other means may be inherited from the parent box. Mechanism arrows that point downward are call arrows. Call arrows enable the sharing of detail between models (linking them together) or between portions of the same model. The called box provides detail for the caller box. Standard arrow positions are shown in Figure 2.2. Supporting information concerning the function and its purpose shall be addressed in the text associated with the diagram. A diagram may or may not have associated text.

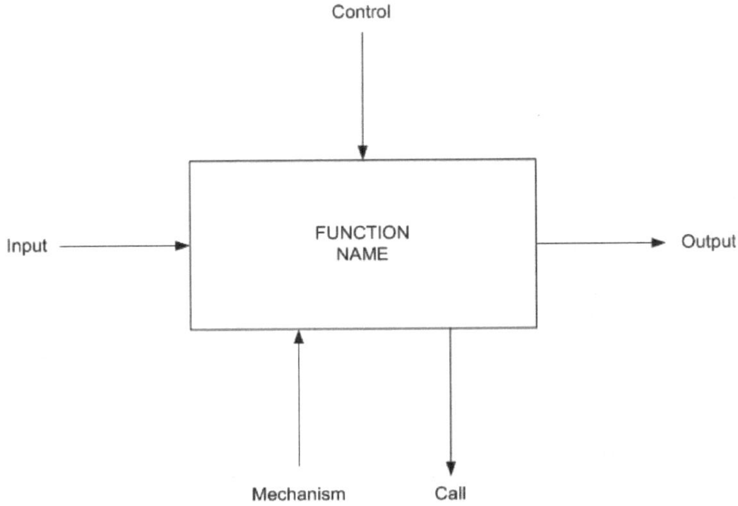

Figure 2.2: Arrow positions and roles

2.3 TYPES OF DIAGRAMS

IDEF0 models are composed of three types of information: graphic diagrams, text, and glossary. These diagram types are cross-referenced to each other. The graphic diagram is the major component of an IDEF0 model, containing boxes, arrows, box/arrow interconnections and associated relationships. Boxes represent each major function of a subject. These functions are broken down or decomposed into more detailed diagrams, until the subject is described at a level necessary to support the goals of a particular project. The top-level diagram in the model provides the most general or abstract description of the subject represented by the model. This diagram is followed by a series of child diagrams providing more detail about the subject.

Each model shall have a top-level context diagram, on which the subject of the model is represented by a single box with its bounding arrows. This is called the A-0 diagram (pronounced A minus zero). The arrows on this diagram interface with functions outside the subject area to establish model focus. Since a single box represents the whole subject, the descriptive name written in the box is general. The same is true for the interface arrows since they also represent the complete set of external interfaces to the subject. The A-0 diagram also sets the model scope or boundary and orientation.

The A-0 context diagram also shall present brief statements specifying the model's viewpoint and purpose, which help to guide and constrain the creation of the model. The viewpoint determines what can be "seen" within the model context, and from what perspective or "slant". Depending on the audience, different statements of viewpoint may be adopted that emphasize different aspects of the subject. Things that are important in one viewpoint may not even appear in a model presented from another viewpoint of the same subject.

The statement of purpose expresses the reason why the model is created and actually determines the structure of the model. The most important features come first in the hierarchy, as the whole top-level function is decomposed into sub-function parts that compose it, and those parts, in turn, are further decomposed until all of the relevant detail of the whole viewpoint is adequately exposed. Each sub-function is modeled individually by a box, with parent boxes detailed by child diagrams at the next lower level. All child diagrams must be within the scope of the top-level context diagram.

Child Diagram

The single function represented on the top-level context diagram may be decomposed into its major sub-functions by creating its child diagram. In turn, each of these subfunctions may be decomposed, each creating another, lower-level child diagram. On a given diagram, some of the functions, none of the functions or all of the functions may be decomposed. Each child diagram contains the child boxes and arrows that provide additional detail about the parent box. The child diagram that results from the decomposition of a function covers the same scope as the parent box it details. Thus, a child diagram may be thought of as being the "inside" of its parent box.

Parent Diagram

A parent diagram is one that contains one or more parent boxes. Every ordinary (noncontext) diagram is also a child diagram, since by definition it details a parent box. Thus a diagram may be both a parent diagram (containing parent boxes) and a child diagram (detailing its own parent box). Likewise, a box may be both a parent box (detailed by a child diagram) and a child box (appearing on a child diagram). The primary hierarchical relationship is between a parent box and the child diagram that details it.

In order to understand better the meanings of Child and Parent diagram, are presented the parent and child diagrams of the material order process.

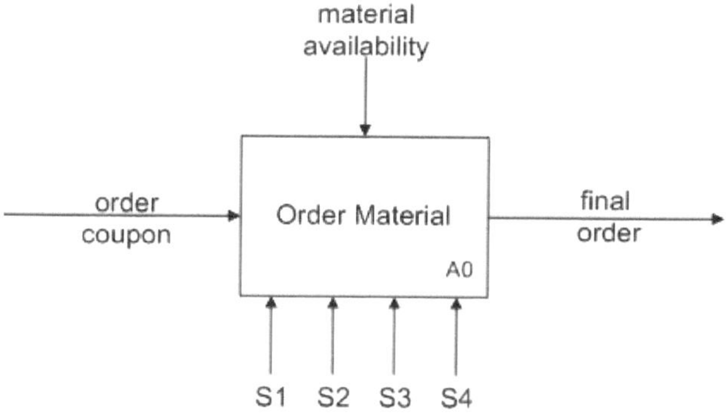

S1: Staff of Management Material and Accoutrement Library Office
S2: Supervisor of Management Material and Accoutrement Library Office
S3: Central Liprary Supervisor
S4: Management Office of Library

Figure 2.3: The contex Diagram of the *Order Of Material* process

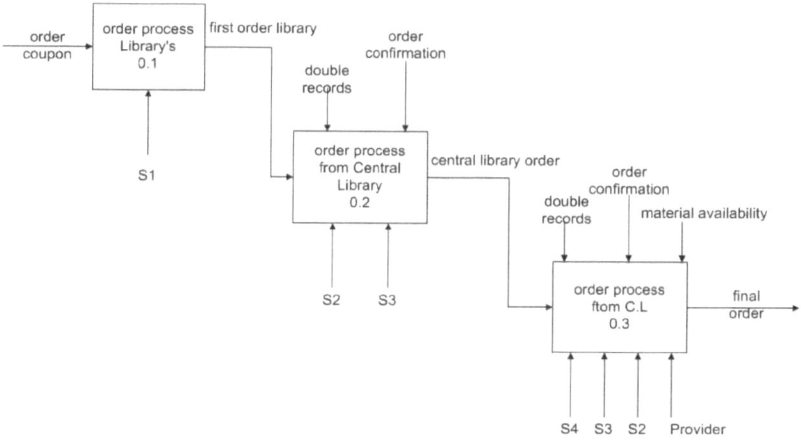

S1: Staff of Management Material and Accoutrement Library Office
S2: Supervisor of Management Material and Accoutrement Library Office
S3: Central Liprary Supervisor
S4: Management Office of Library

Figure 2.4: First level model of the *Order of Material* process

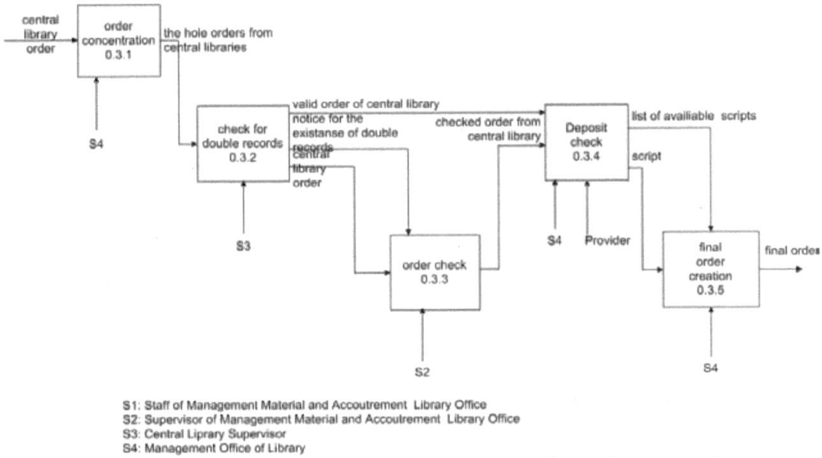

Figure 2.5: Second level model of the *Order of Material* process

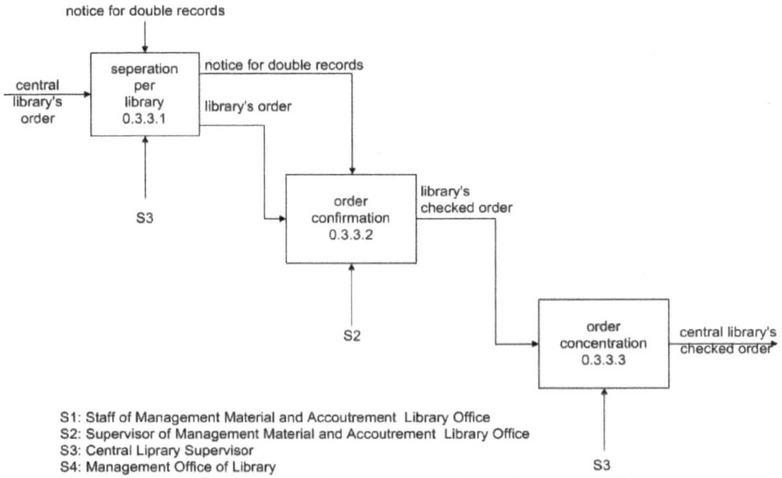

Figure 2.6: Forth Level of the *Order of Material* process

As we can see above, the diagram in Figure 2.3 is the parent diagram of the process *Order Material*. The diagram in Figure 2.4 is the child diagram of A0, in Figure 2.5 we can see the child diagram of 0.3 and finally in Figure we see the diagram of 0.3.3. in Figure 2.4 the process *Order Material* is divided into sub processes. In Figure 2.5 the process *Order Material from Central Library* is divided into sub processes and lastly in Figure 2.6 the process *Order Check* is divided into sub processes. In that way we achieve the division of the whole process that is under study into different levels that we want to study at each time.

2.4 IDEF0 CONCEPTS

The IDEF0's objective is to efficiently describe complex business processes and systems as well as to promote effective communication between the modellers and the process' participants. The IDEF0 model provides structured format and syntax to facilitate user communication. An activity is described by a box labelled with a verb. Each activity may have inputs, controls, outputs and mechanisms (ICOMs). Several activity boxes and related Inputs, Controls, Outputs, and Mechanisms construct an IDEF0 model. Thus, an IDEF0 model describes the individual activities of a process as well as the interrelationships between these activities: for example the output of one activity may be the input, control, or even mechanism of another activity within the same model.

The IDEF0 model supports the hierarchical decomposition of activities. A box in an IDEF0 model represents the boundaries of an activity. Inside the box there is the decomposition of this activity in sub activities. This hierarchical structure supports increasing level of detail by hiding unnecessary complexity and revealing it when is needed to enable a better and deeper understanding.

In this way the first step in constructing an IDEF0 model is to create a Context Diagram. A Context Diagram limits the scope of the modelling effort. It represents the function, inputs, outputs, controls and mechanism at the highest level. Then a functional decomposition of the context diagram follows.

It should be mentioned that an IDEF0 model just depicts what an organisation does, but it does not support the specification of how the work is done in terms of specific logic or the timing associated with the activities. The abstraction away from timing, sequencing and decision logic allows concision in an IDEF0 model. In fact, the model's lack of reliance on time is the most powerful feature of it, since it provides an objective assessment of what actually occurs in the process.

IDEF0's standard notation, it's hierarchical structuring and the effective rules for decomposition facilitates learning and understanding of the modelled process. One problem with the IDEF0 models is that sometimes they are so concise that it is difficult for someone non-expert to understand them. Moreover, the abstraction away from timing, sequencing, and decision logic, also contributes to comprehension difficulties among readers who tend to interpret IDEF0 models as representing a sequence of activities.

IDEF0 allows the modeller to express clearly factors, which are required by an activity (inputs, controls, mechanisms). Therefore, it provides the information necessary to generate activity-based costing scenarios. By analysing the "as-is" situation of the process and focusing on high-cost activities, the methodology identifies prime candidates for reengineering.

However, IDEF0 models are imprecise about details at the primitive process element stage and vague about details of concurrency, resource conflict, timing, and state-oriented behaviour. As a result they should be extended to allow execution or enactment. Most models of this category cannot be simulated or enacted due to the necessity to add more information than the notation supports.

Moreover, since the model describes what an organisation does, it is good in identifying the core activities and secondary functions of the organisation. It provides the modeller and process participants with the means to understand the structure of activities within a process, it is a useful device in radical change BPR efforts, where the concern is to understand a process as a whole and in particular what is done rather who does it and how.

Having the above in mind we can conclude that the IDEF0 model could facilitate the communication between the modellers and the process participant's as well as their understanding of the process by being used in high level modelling of the current situation. It could also be used to create high-level models of the "to-be" process.

2.5 INTRODUCTION TO IDEF3

The IDEF3 Process Description Capture Method was created specifically to capture descriptions of sequences of activities. The primary goal of IDEF3 is to provide a structured method by which a domain expert can express knowledge about the operation of a particular system or organization. Knowledge acquisition is enabled by direct capture of assertions about real-world processes and events in a form that is most natural for capture. This includes the capture of assertions about the objects that participate in the process, assertions about supporting objects, and the precedence and causality relations between processes and events in the environment.

IDEF3 supports this kind of knowledge acquisition by providing a reliable and well structured approach for process knowledge acquisition, and an expressively powerful, yet easy-to-use, language for information capture and expression. These two dimensions of IDEF3—the procedure embodying proven practices and an expressively powerful language—work together to focus user attention on relevant aspects of a given process and provide the expressive power necessary to explicitly represent information about the nature and structure of that process.

An IDEF3 Process Description is developed using two knowledge acquisition strategies: a *process-centered* strategy and an *object-centered* strategy. The process-centered strategy organizes process knowledge with a focus on processes and their temporal, causal, and logical relations within a scenario. The second dimension organizes process knowledge with its focus on objects and their state change behavior in a single scenario or across multiple scenarios.

Using one or both of these process knowledge acquisition strategies, IDEF3 users develop IDEF3 Process Descriptions. Both strategies use the basic elements of the IDEF3 language to capture and express the assertions that form the description. Graphical projections of the information contained in process descriptions are created using IDEF3's graphical language. These graphical projections—used to both record process information directly and as a mechanism to display process information—are called *schematics*.

Two types of IDEF3 schematics parallelize the two process knowledge acquisition strategies. The IDEF3 *Process Schematic* displays a process-centered view of a scenario. *Object Schematics* support the graphical display of object-centered information. Object Schematics that display an object-centered view of a single scenario are called *Transition Schematics*. Transition Schematics that display additional objects and object relations to provide context-setting information are called *Enhanced Transition Schematics*. Object Schematics that display object-centered information spanning multiple scenarios are simply called *Object Schematics*.

An IDEF3 Process Description may contain zero or more Process Schematics and zero or more Object Schematics. For example, recording that participants in a domain recognize a particular object, is considered part of the description of that domain. An object so identified may or may not have an Object

Schematic associated with it in a description. Yet these objects are considered part of the description. The scenario concept is used to organize both the process-centered and object-centered views. The collection of scenarios and the information they serve to organize *is* the IDEF3 Process Description.

2.6 THE PROCESS SCHEMATICS

IDEF3 Process Schematics are the primary means for capturing, managing, and displaying process-centered knowledge. These schematics provide a graphical medium that helps domain experts and analysts from different application areas communicate knowledge about processes. This includes knowledge about events and activities, the objects that participate in those occurrences, and the constraining relations that govern the behavior of an occurrence.

A process-centered description is constructed systematically, using the basic building blocks of the IDEF3 schematic language, linked together in different ways. These building blocks have specific semantics associated with them. That is, they are used to represent certain kinds of activities or relations in the real world. In Figure 2.7 we have an example of a Process Semantic.

The small box containing the "X" denotes a *junction.* A junction is a point in the process where a process splits into multiple paths, or where multiple paths merge. Junctions represent constraints (or the effects of constraints) of the *activation logic* for the process. For example, the first junction in the above figure indicates that only one path will be taken in an activation of the described process.

The IDEF3 method allows users to capture descriptions at varying levels of abstraction by providing a mechanism called decomposition. Decomposition provides a means of organizing a more detailed description of a UOB.

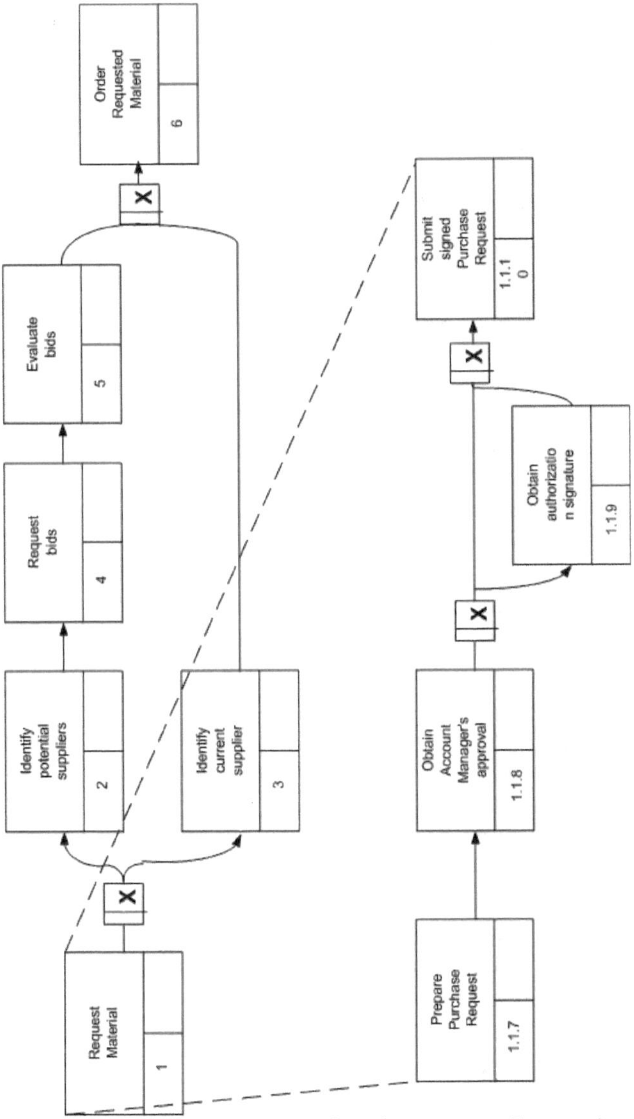

Figure 2.7: Example of a Process Semantic

The decomposition schematic follows the same syntactic rules as those for a scenario and is created using the same IDEF3 elements. A UOB can have any number of different decompositions, all on the same level. The use of, more than one, decomposition for the same UOB is for the purpose of representing different points of view or providing greater details of the processing relating to the UOB.

The UOB *Request Material* in Figure 2.7 has been *decomposed* into UOBs 7 through 10. The numbers in the lower-left corner of UOB boxes 7 through 10 include a reference to UOB 1 (the first digit) and the decomposition (decomposition 1 of UOB 1). This is illustrative of the IDEF3 numbering scheme, which allows explicit trace ability between levels of detail in the description. The process description depicted in Figure 2.7 shows the material ordering process from a particular point of view—that of the business owner. It is possible to conceive of other views for this process—for example, that of the Account Manager. Each view to be described would be presented in a separate decomposition with a unique label and number.

2.7 THE OBJECT SCHEMATICS

IDEF3 Object Schematics capture, manage, and display *object-centered* descriptions of a process—that is, information about how objects of various kinds are transformed into other kinds of things through a process, how objects of a given kind change states through a process, or context-setting information about important relations among objects in a process. In IDEF3, an object is any physical or conceptual thing that is recognized and referred to by participants in the domain as a part of their descriptions of what happens in their domain. Correctly identifying, characterizing, and naming objects is a necessary step in the creation of object-centred IDEF3 Process Descriptions. Object names are often nouns or noun phrases that may or may not be coupled with a state descriptor.

Object Schematics may be developed in the context of a single scenario, thus characterizing the state transitions traversed by participating objects in an occurrence of the scenario. These schematics, called Transition Schematics, allow users to specify the rules that govern the transitions between object states in a scenario occurrence. Alternatively, Object Schematics may evolve in a more opportunistic fashion, capturing descriptions of objects, object states, and their transitions across multiple scenarios. Object Schematics developed in this fashion make no attempt to define the structure for object state change behavior in a scenario occurrence. This cross-scenario

Object Schematic development approach is often useful when exploring what object-centered process information merits a more detailed focus or when attempting to discover context-setting information about the objects encountered in a description. Object Schematics may be distinguished from the more specialized Transition Schematics (and Enhanced Transition Schematics) by the absence of a context-setting scenario name Generally speaking; IDEF3 Object Schematics are developed to provide an object-centered description of a particular process or scenario. Transition Schematics therefore tend to dominate the attention of those developing IDEF3 Object Schematics. In Figure 2.8 is represented an Object Schematic for the *Order Material* scenario derived from the business owner's description.

One of the first steps to develop an Object Schematic is to identify the possible states in which the object can exist. Though a real-world object often evolves through a continuum of states, an Object Schematic focuses on those distinguished states of particular interest to the domain expert.

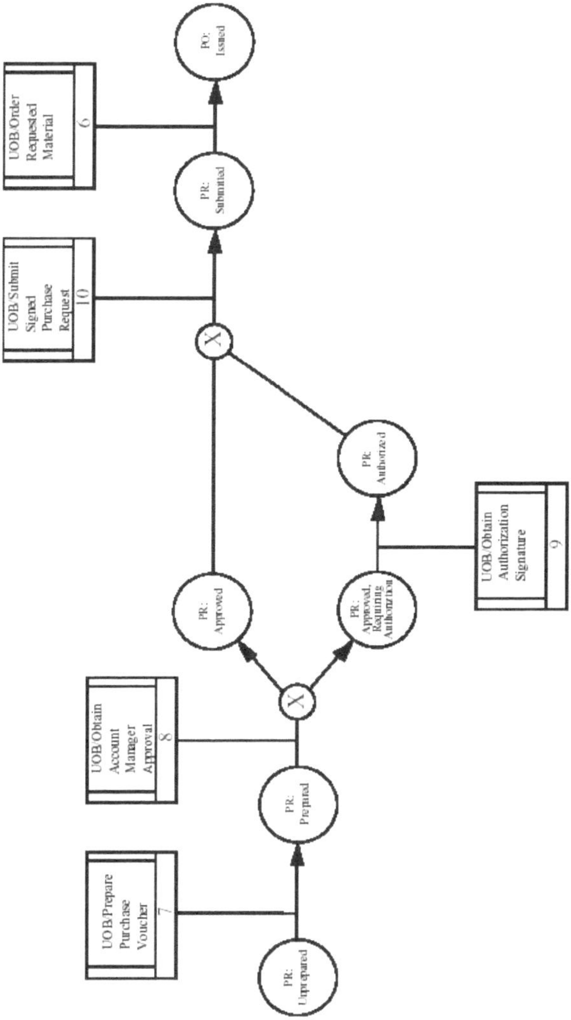

Figure 2.8: Example of a Transition Schematic

The transition arcs (arrows with triangular, filled-in heads) connecting the circles symbolize a *state transition*, the activity of changing from one state to another. The conditions that establish when an object is in a given state, how it exists a state, how it can transition between states, and how it can enter a new state are recorded on a special form.

The banded boxes linked to the arrows (called *referents*) are aids to describe the relationships between objects states and UOBs, scenarios, or other Transition Schematics that participate in a scenario occurrence. UOBs, scenarios, and other Transition Schematics that participate in a transition between states, are indicated, by attaching appropriately labeled referents to the Object Schematic. The relative positioning of referents on the Transition Schematic indicates the order in which they occur. IDEF3 is intended as a mechanism for structuring the assertions made by the domain expert. It does not force the completion of partial information with modeling assumptions.

The schematic in Figure 2.8 may be embellished to include additional context-setting information. An example of this is provided in Figure 2.9. In this figure, the Transition Schematic has been supplemented with objects and appropriate relation links that provide additional information. For example, the three-place relation that stands between the kinds PR: Prepared, Direct Project, and Authorization Signature indicates that Purchase Requests involving Direct Projects require an authorization signature. Furthermore, an Authorization Signature is included on each Purchase Request that has been authorized. The schematic also indicates that a Requester may not be the same individual who approves or authorizes a Purchase Request.

The basic syntactic elements of the IDEF3 process description language are shown in Figures 2.10 (a, b, c), which was used in the above figures.

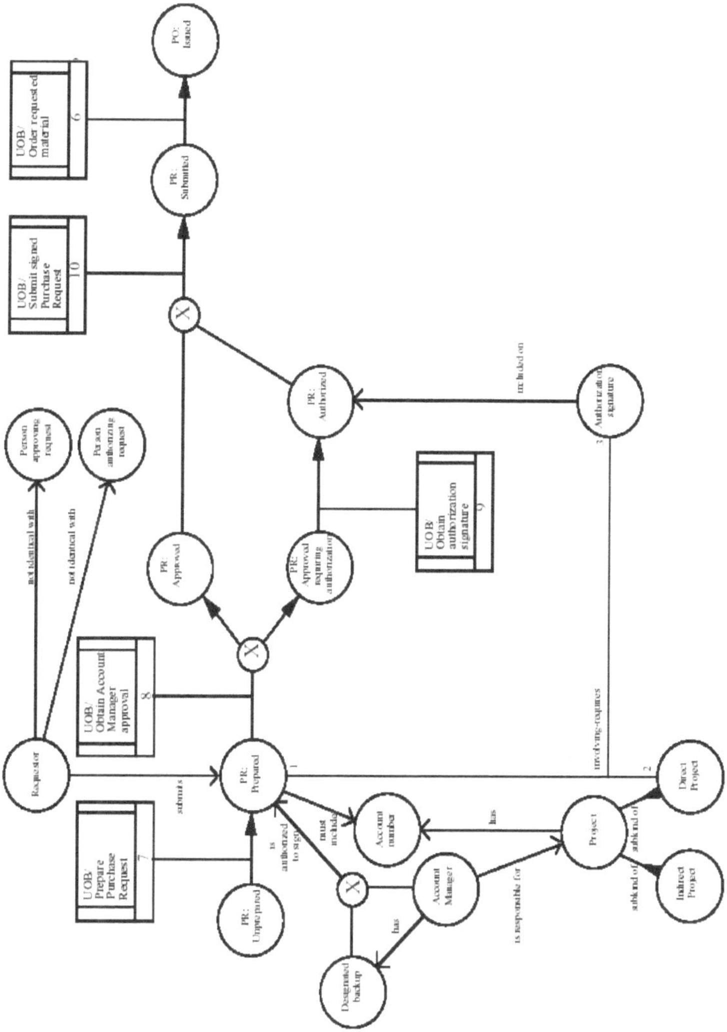

Figure 2.9: Example of an Enhanced Transition Schematic

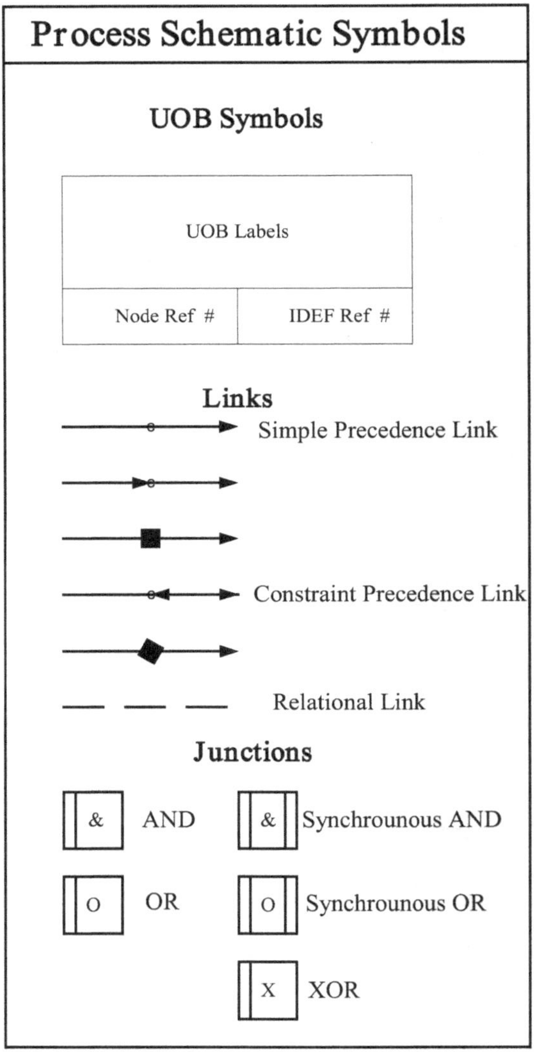

Figure 2.10 (a): Symbols used for IDEF3 Process Description Schematics

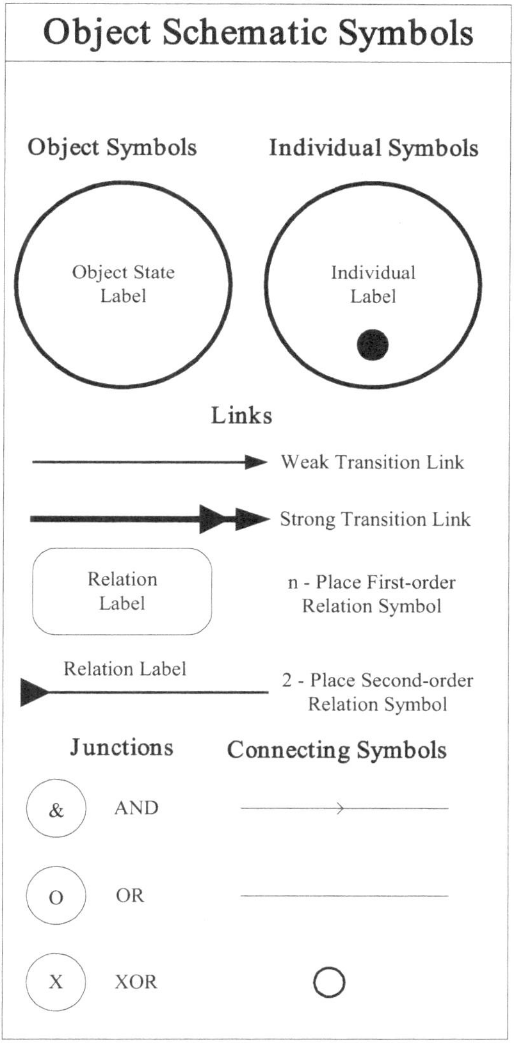

Figure 2.10 (b): Symbols used for IDEF3 Process Description Schematics

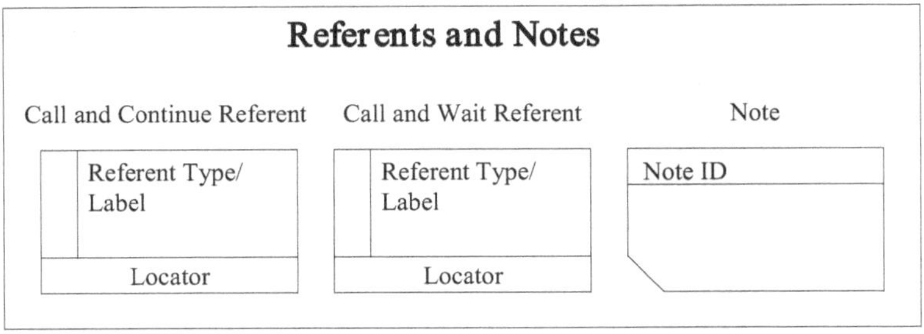

Figure 2.10 (c): Symbols used for IDEF3 Process Description Schematics

2.8 IDEF3 CONCEPTS

The IDEF3 Process Description capture method, captures all temporal information including precedence and causality relationships associated with enterprise processes, in a form natural to domain experts by providing a structured method for expressing knowledge about how a process works. It builds structured descriptions (Unlike simulation languages that build predictive mathematical models). These descriptions capture information about what a system actually does or will do and also provide for the organisation and expression of different user views of the system.

Process schematics are the most familiar and broadly used components of IDEF3 and they provide a visualisation mechanism for process-centred descriptions of a scenario. The graphical elements that comprise process schematics include Unit of Behaviour *(UOB)* boxes, precedence links, junctions, referents, and notes. Referents and notes are constructs that are common across process and object schematics.

A *UOB* describes a type of situation; an instance of a UOB is simply an occurrence of the UOB. A process description represents the types of situations (processes, functions, etc.) that can occur in the system and the logical and temporal constraints that bind them together. Links connect UOB boxes to form representations of dynamic processes. They are primarily used to denote significant relationships among UOBs like temporal, logical, causal, natural and conventional. Junctions provide a mechanism to specify the logic of process branching. Additionally, junctions simplify the capture of timing and sequencing relationships between multiple process paths. Referents are used to enhance understanding, provide additional meaning, and simplify the construction of both process schematics and object schematics.

IDEF3 supports decomposition of a UOB at any level of detail and in different ways in order to manage complexity. It thus enables to model the same process from different knowledge sources or different points of view. This capability is also useful in domain situations where a given process involves multiple functional organisations. The IDEF3 method was designed to be easy to learn and use by individuals having little or no training in structured techniques. A designer can easily learn using the method in order to built descriptions of different scenarios of a process. On the other hand, the descriptions built using the method are not so straightforward for the process participants to understand them, and as a consequence they do not enable the communication between them

2.9 USING IDEF0 WITH IDEF3

IDEF3 is not intended to be a replacement for IDEF0. If the system being analyzed is very large (e.g., Manufacture Aerospace Product), precedence relations may not be evident. In these cases, it is often better to start with an IDEF0 model. Such a model can then be decomposed to a level where the precedence relations among activities become prominent. On the other hand, if the facts collected can be organized into a cohesive story, it is generally better to formulate the IDEF3 process description first, and then abstract an IDEF0 model from that description.

The IDEF3 method was designed with this interaction in mind. The IDEF3 syntax recognizes this relationship by providing a means of referencing associated IDEF0 activities from within the IDEF3 UOB. All UOB boxes have a field (see lower right of Figure 2.11) for providing a reference to an activity in an IDEF0 model, or comparable function or process model (e.g., a node in a Logical Data Flow Diagram or HIPO chart).

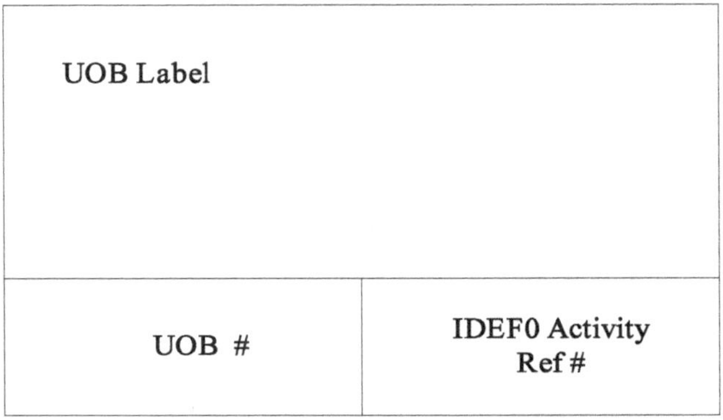

Figure 2.11: Unit of Behavior Fields

The reference scheme in IDEF3 assumes that zero, one, or many IDEF0 activities will map onto a single UOB. In cases where the UOB maps to only part of an IDEF0 activity, the activity referent should point to the set of child activities in the IDEF0 model that is actually involved. If the IDEF0 model is not defined to a low enough level of detail, the extent of the mapping should be described in the UOB elaboration. As UOBs are identified, IDEF0 references should be included.

IDEF3 integrates very well with IDEF0. The IDEF0 method can be used to build high level models of business process by abstracting away from timing, sequencing and decision logic. The IDEF3 method takes the knowledge captured in IDEF0, supplements it with a process owner's real-world knowledge of how a process works, and produces accurate process scenarios. These scenarios can be used to see in detail the process under study. Due to the method's formal semantics and syntax, the produced scenarios can feed directly into simulation scenarios.

2.10 SUMMARIZATION

IDEF diagrams provide a mechanism for analysing and documenting processes. They are designed to model decisions, actions and activities of an organization or a system. IDEF modelling is a very effective tool for communication between the analyst and the participants of the process. IDEF diagrams show activities explicitly. Entities are shown with the data flow, whilst resources are presented implicitly, throughout the mechanisms. They cannot represent all the elements important for simulation modelling, such as queues, random behaviour and process dynamics, but could provide the basic elements for simulation environment [VBGGVH 03].

The IDEF0 method is designed to model the decisions, actions and activities of an organization or another system and is targeted to communicating and analysing the functional perspective of a system [RMPBPBMP 98]. The activity (or function) is represented by boxes; inputs are represented by the arrows flowing into the left hand side of an activity box; outputs are represented by arrows flowing out the right hand side of an activity box; the arrows flowing into the top portion of the box represent constraints or controls on the activities; and the final element represented by arrows flowing into the bottom of the activity box are the mechanisms that carry out the activity [May 92]. Perhaps the main strength of IDEF0 is its simplicity, as it uses – as I mentioned above – only one notational construct, called the ICOM (Input – Control – Output – Mechanism) [VBGGVH 03].

We can say that IDEF3 is a technique used to produce a dynamic model of the system, as it can produce two views of the system; a process-centred view and an object-centred view

[CBMBCF 02]. IDEF3 describes processes, as ordered sequences of events or activities. As such, IDEF3 is a scenario-driven process flow modelling technique, based on the direct capture of precedence and causality relations between situations and events [RMPBPBMP 98]. The goal of an IDEF3 model is to provide a structured method for expressing the domain expert's knowledge about how a particular system or organization works (as opposed to IDEF0, which is mainly concerned with what activities the organization performs). Similar to IDEF0, the main strength of IDEF3, is the simplicity of its notation, which relies on only one basic construct, called the UOB (Unit of Behaviour) [VBGGVH 03]. The Units of Behaviours represent types of happenings (such as events, acts, and e.t.c.) and describes the actual detailed in the box. The other basic elements of IDEF3 are Junctions and Links. Links connect the boxes and describe the relationships between the various UOBs. Junctions explicitly describe the logic of multiple links either coming together or spreading apart.

One characteristic of the IDEF0 modelling technique is that each activity and the arrows can be decomposed (or exploded) into more detailed level of analysis. This characteristic is especially useful in enterprise modelling where details about lower level activities can be captured, but at the same time, be hidden from models of the enterprise at higher more abstract levels. The IDEF3 method does not explicitly limit the number of activities which can exist within a given process model [LWBHAP 97]. This means that a process could be represented within one level of abstraction using the IDEF3 method, while using the IDEF0 technique, multiple decompositions of the system model are required.

3

SWIMLANE DIAGRAMS

3.1 INTRODUCTION

Swimlane diagrams have become very popular because they highlight the relevant variables in a simple notation that requires little or no training to understand. They can show an entire business process from the beginning to the end. They can show a process at any level, from a very high view to one showing each individual task. Swimlane diagrams, with slight variations, go by many names:

- Process map,
- Process Responsibility Diagram (PRD),
- Responsibility Process Matrix (RPM),
- Functional deployment chart,
- People-process chart,
- Line Of Visibility (LON) chart,
- Activity diagram in Unified Modeling Language (UML).

In order to define the flow of information and control in a business process, the three Rs are defined: Roles, Responsibilities, Routes:

- *Roles*: Are the actors or process performers in the process,
- *Responsibilities*: Are the individual tasks that each actor is responsible for,

- *Routes*: Are the workflows and decisions that connect the tasks together, and therefore define the path that an individual work item will take through the process.

3.2 ACTORS AND ROLES

Each actor in the process gets its own labeled Swimlane, delineated by dotted lines. There is no practical difference between an *actor* and a *role*. An actor is any identifiable person or group that handles the work between the initial event and the achievement of the process's result.

An actor could be a role played by a person in an organization such as an external customer or supplier, or it could be a job function normally assumed by a single person or a job title held by many. Sometimes the actor is an organization unit such as company, division, department or work unit, but in rare cases it could even be another process. Actors could be automated devices or Information Systems.

The actors in the Swimlane are listed down the left side of the diagram, and to each one, is given a swimlane that extends left to right across the page (Figure 3.1).

In Figure 3.1, all of the work performed by an actor appears in that actor's swimlane. Some swimlanes are wider than others, because of complex branching or parallel tasks performed by that actor. Actors can appear from top to bottom in their order of appearance or the order of importance to the process, or even alphabetically. Many modelers always put the customer first, and the systems last, with the orders in some logical order.

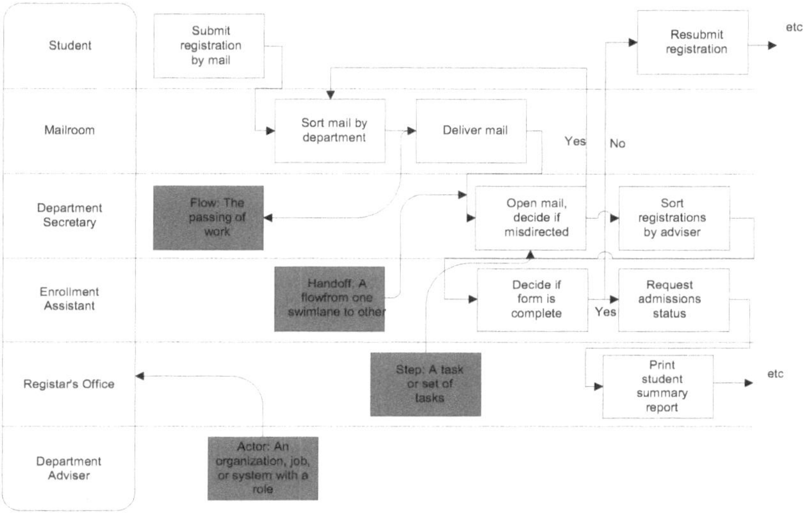

Figure 3.1: A swimlane diagram includes actors, tasks, flow, and handoffs.

3.2.1 How to choose an actor

In some situations a single person can perform multiple roles in a process in which case each role should be given a separate swimlane. In these situations we must place the swimlanes adjacent to one another, and provide some indication that the same actor (person) performs them all.

All the actors must be depicted; we cannot simplify or summarize actors, as it is very important to see all the handoffs. When we have different roles in the same department, again we show all the distinct roles because they do different tasks and there are handoffs. In this point we have an exception. If the are not different roles but different job titles, perhaps based on seniority, but they all perform the same tasks, in that case can be combined as one actor.

A system or a device, if it is doing a significant step (or actually does a step), we must give it its own swimlane. At this point it is critical to remember that: *every actor in the process that holds work, moves the work along or introduces delay*, must be shown in the swimlane [SMcD 01]. Devices such as ATMs and IVR (Interactive Voice Response) systems might be considered to be actors because they take control and add value. An ATM also holds work for subsequent processing, so it can be said to introduce delay. On the other hand an information system that assists a human in completing a step (task), such as an Internet – based order system entry, would not be treated as an actor, however it could be mentioned in the step name, such as "Create order using Web site".

Likewise, an inanimate physical object like an inbox can be shown as an actor, generally completing the step "*hold work*". These kinds of actors can hold the work independently of any other actor, and certainly introduce delay. One of advantages of doing this is that it makes more visually apparent when the process's work item is waiting. It also gives us the opportunity to ask how and when the work item gets to the inbox and how and when it leaves. Examples of inanimate objects that could be added to a diagram, include:

- An inbox or outbox where items await attention or transport,
- A tub file where problem cases are left until time is allocated to resolve them,
- The order board.

Things like the telephone network cannot be shown, because it is more or less instantaneous. Further more we do not show the e-mail server, but we could show an e-mail inbox if it holds the work (actors do not check it instantly). Moreover we do not show something that holds work but it is under control of another actor (e.g. a delivery card).

A process could be an actor in another process, if it is a process we depend on, or a process we hand off to. It is not a usual situation, but if we hand off work to separate process and wait for something to come back from it, the process itself is an actor. It is a need to have a swimlane for other processes that our process interacts with if the other process performs work that our process waits for. We must be sure that the other process is really an independent one, not activities that should be treated as part of the process being studied. A swimlane is not necessary if our process does not expect a response.

3.3 PROCESS STEPS AND RESPONSIBILITIES

A step is a task or set of tasks performed by an actor. They are also called responsibilities, activities, actions, or other names, but the usual name is “steps” or “tasks”. Steps are shown on the swimlane diagram as a labeled box in the lane of the actor performing it, as we can see in Figure 3.1. Steps can involve multiple actors; meeting and assist are situations in which two or more actors are required (Figure 3.2). As it is shown in Figure 3.2, the step “Resolve order discrepancy”, involves all the three actors, whereas the step “Develop production schedule” involves the actors Production Planning and Delivery Logistics.

It is very difficult to decide which steps to include in our model at any time. The first thing to remember is that our objective goal is to model a specific process, not all of the activity a person or a department is responsible for.

The swimlane diagram must be very simple so that anyone who reads it should be able to understand and follow it. To ensure simplicity, some guidelines for naming a process step must be followed. The step name is in verb – noun format but often includes additional detail. The text box for a step is a description, that tell us *how* to do it. The components of a step name are:

- ✓ Action verb (Assign, Sort, e.t.c.),
- ✓ Optional Qualifier (Replacement, Initial, e.t.c.),
- ✓ Object (Payment, Service Request, e.t.c.),
- ✓ Information on how (by Fax, on Form, e.t.c.).

Another guideline to follow is that the step name should convey the result achieved by the step, such as:

- Name – Receive AB Application
- Result – AB Application is Received
- Name – Issue AB
- Result – AB is Issued

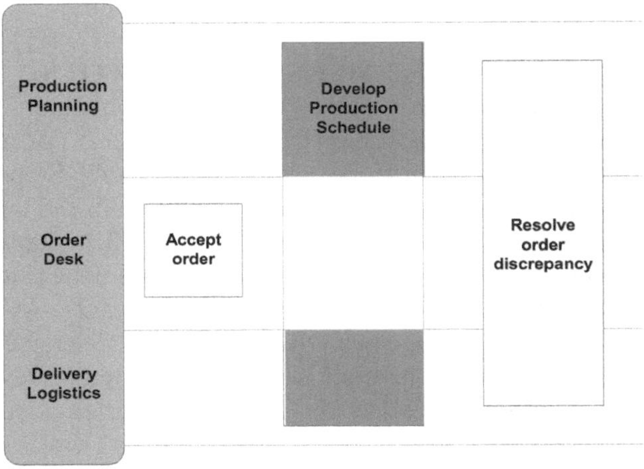

Figure 3.2: Illustrating process steps performed by multiple actors

3.3.1 How to choose a process step

It is very critical in swimlane diagram designing, the number of steps that should be included as well as who are these steps. In order to avoid these difficult situations we must follow the mantra: "*Show every step that adds value; moves the work along; or introduces delay*" [SMcD 01]. The first guideline "*Adds Value*", could be stated as "causes a state chorng in the direction of completion". Strictly speaking it could also subtract value or cause a state change in the opposite direction of completion. In either case, work is being performed on the work item, which includes inspection or validation activities.

The guideline "Moves the work along" indicates that some steps may not change the work item in any way, except to transport it between other steps in the workflow. The internal or external delivery services that handle the work item must always be shown. Finally the guideline “Introduces delay” covers the situation that a step may not change the state of the work item or move it along, but some subsequent step could not proceed until the delay – introducing step completes.

As mentioned above, some steps move a work item, some enter or display data, some make decisions, and some add value by transforming the work item in some way. Every step is a simple box and we are doing that because the simpler we keep the diagram the greater the number of people who will be willing to look at it. We trade simplicity and participation for precision and detail.

3.4 FLOWS AND ROUTES

Flow is the passing of work from one step to the next, shown as lines with arrowheads. Flow is also known as routes, events, communications, and transitions. Sometimes accomplishing the flow may actually be a step in its self such as “Retrieve tray from mailroom”. A handoff is a special kind of flow from one swimlane to another that is from one actor to the other. Handoffs are a focus for process analysis because they are often a source for delay, or errors or expense in the process.

The flow line that connects two process steps means that when the first step (task) completes, then the second step begins or can begin. There often multiple flow lines into a step that all must occur before the step can begin. In Figure 3.3 is represented the way that the flow lines were drawn.

In Figure 3.3 when step B follows step A, then the flow line is leaving the step (step A) from right and is entering step B from the left. An exception, is returning or looping takes place, where the flow line enter from the to or the bottom. Real processes exhibit complex flows, which can be characterized as one of the four following types [SMcD 01]:

- ✓ Sequential flow,

- ✓ Parallel flow,
- ✓ Concurrent flow,
- ✓ Conditional flow.

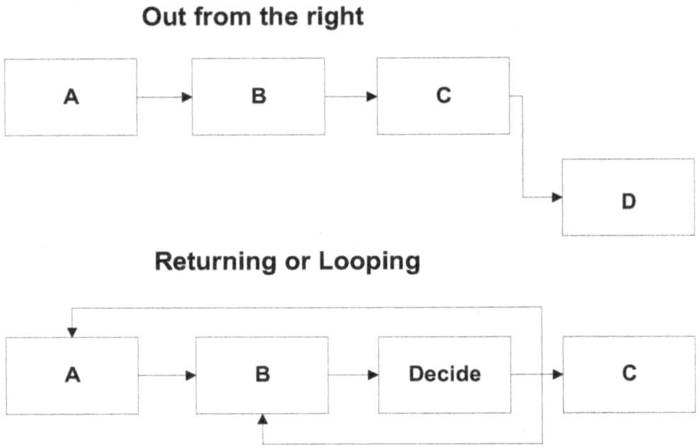

Figure 3.3: Conventions for flow

In a Sequential flow, which is the simpler case, the work proceeds from one step to the next process step in order. In Parallel flow two or more step (or sequences of steps) proceed independently. In Concurrent flow, two or more steps must proceed at the same time, whereas in Conditional flow a step or sequence of steps may or may not be accomplished at all, depending on the conditions. The non-sequential flow (e.g. conditional flow), lead to various forms of branching.

3.4.1 Branching in flows

With a conditional flow occurs the basic branch, when a decision is made which directs the workflow to one or more alternative flows (Figure 3.4). The decision is indicated by the usage of the decision. In Figure 3.4 when a branch (decision) is depicted, some basic key points must be followed:

- ❖ There is exactly one flow line leaving the decision symbol, which then splits into two or more branches,

- The most common case is showed as the top branch,
- Each branch is labeled to indicate which decision outcome will follow that path,
- The branches are mutually exclusive, only one is followed.

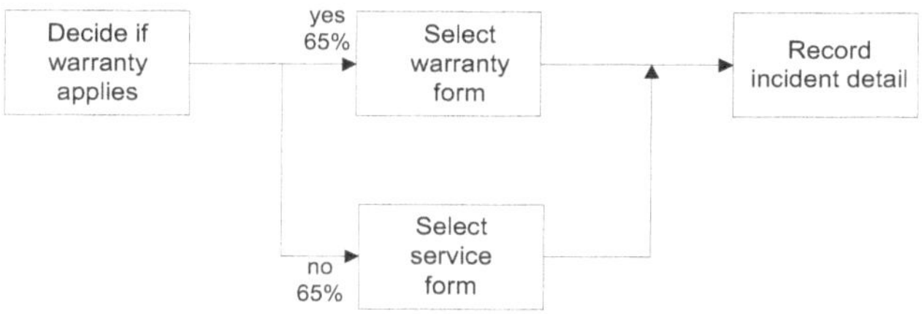

Figure 3.4: Branching

3.4.2 Multiple flows

In parallel or in concurrent flows there are multiple flow lines leaving a step. There are different types of branches, so specific symbols in order to indicate this severalty must be added. In Figure 3.5, a fork can have on of three qualifiers, an "AND branch", an "OR branch (or LOGICAL OR branch)" or an "EXCLUSIVE OR branch (or XOR branch)".

In the AND branch all the forks will be followed and their steps must be accomplished eventually. In the OR branch one or more forks (at least one) will be followed. Finally in an XOR branch exactly one of the forks will be taken, which corresponds to our "decide".

What the flow line really means is, the precedence and the dependence. The step at the arrowhead cannot go the other until the step at other end has been completed. It is very important to accurately show the "input flows" that are necessary for a step to begin, as well as the "output flows" that terminate a process step.

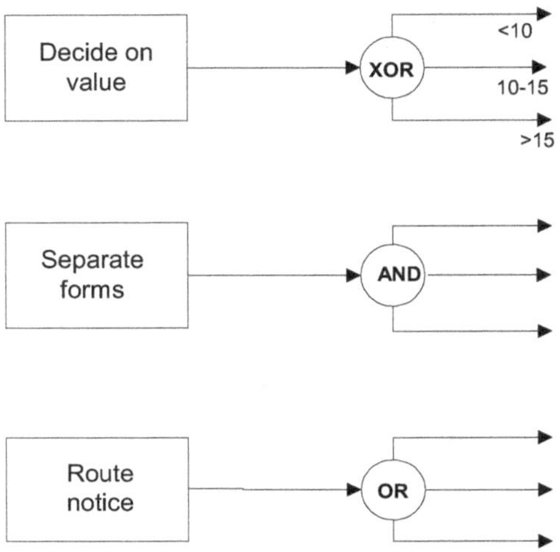

Figure 3.5: Multiple flows

3.5 HOW TO PERFORM SWIMLANE DIAGRAMS

As Figure 3.1 shows, it is very easy to read a properly done swimlane diagram but it is very difficult to produce it, because many situations arise that are not obvious how to depict. In order to make a properly swimlane diagram a modeler must take into consideration the topics mentioned above. A modeler must depict the actors that are involved, the steps (tasks) that they accomplish and the flow of work between them.

The actors are listed down the left side of the diagram and each one is given a swimlane that extends left to right across the page. The steps are shown as boxes in the swimlane of the actor who performs them. Flows show which actor performs a given step but also what previous step must be accomplished before that step can begin. Swimlane diagrams do not try to depict multiple work items at a time, but they trace the path of a single work item or transaction as it flows through the process.

In order to control the addition of detail, three levels of detail for swimlane diagrams are defined [SMcD 01]:

- Level 1 or handoff level diagram, Level 2 or flow level diagram,
- Level 3 or task level diagram.

Level 1

It is the initial model and the most important. It is the handoff level diagram and its purpose is to highlight handoffs. Every handoff is shown, but detail about the steps is absolutely minimized, each time an actor is involved in a process no matter how large or how small the contribution, it is shown as a single box. Thus it has only one step (box) each time there is contiguous or uninterrupted work by an actor from receiving a handoff (starting a task) to initiating the final handoff for that work item (completing a task). An actor may have many steps in the handoff diagram if each one takes place at a different time in the process.

Handoff diagrams highlight each point in the process where an actor is involved. They simplify the steps greatly but not the actors, every single actor in the process is shown. The corollary is that as we progress through subsequent levels of detail we add steps, not actors. Each handoff is a source of delay, error, expense, so it is a tremendous benefit for us from a diagram (handoff diagram) to make process timing and dynamics visible.

Level 2

Is the milestone level diagram, used to understand the key steps that determine flow or impact overall performance? It is a more detailed level than level 1 is. In order to built a good level 2 diagram we must add the following steps to handoff diagram, to illustrate:

- Decisions that affect the flow in a significant way,
- Significant looping,
- The mechanisms of any handoffs that introduce delay, errors, expense.

A level 2 diagram, is usually three to five times as large as the level 1 diagram. If at this point we can understand our process we can stop modeling, so there is no need to proceed to level 3 diagram.

Level 3

The previous levels show what happens but they do not show much detail on how. Level 3 makes the transition into describing the details of how the process is implemented. It contains individual steps, and details which characterize how the workflow is implemented. It shows the mechanisms of any handoffs not shown in previous levels.

3.6 UNIFIED MODELING LANGUAGE (UML)

As mentioned in chapter one, a model is an abstract representation of a specification, a design or a system, from a particular point of view. It is often represented visually (IDEF diagrams, Petri Nets, Activity Diagrams), by one ore more diagrams. It aims to express the essentials without giving unnecessary detail. Its purpose is to enable people involved in the development to think about and discuss about the problems and the solutions. A model in order to be useful must have a precise and understood meaning.

A modeling language is a way of expressing the various models produced during the development process. A modeling language defines a collection of model elements, is normally diagrammatic and could be text based. It has:

- *Syntax*: In a diagram-based modeling language, the rules that determine which diagram is legal,
- *Semantics*: The rules that determine what a legal diagram means.

Both syntax and semantics can be given more or less formally. There are some modeling languages but the Unified Modeling Language (UML) is one of the most promising. UML is an object oriented modeling language standardized by the

Object Management Group (OMG) in 1997. [OMG 00]. Different companies have provided a huge amount of UML supporting tools, because UML is a totally independent standard. At first UML was designed for system and software development but later was extended towards to different areas of modeling including of course the business process modeling [HEMP 98].

The notation of UML is very clear and easy to learn even to inexperienced users. UML diagrams can be understood without big efforts of study. We can say that the UML diagrams fit well to many purposes and areas under study. UML suites (fits) particularly to business process modeling, because UML supports a visualization of actions and activities that are being performed in an organization or an enterprise. The processes can be modeled in more detail for further analysis, redesign and automation. The processes can be divided into sub processes and the important actions or parts can be modeled in more detail. Additionally UML can represent synchronization and parallelism of actions and both human and IT-roles in collaboration. Object orientation in common allows the models to be comprehensive, understandable, changeable, adaptable and reusable [HSTJPO 02].

A process can be represented through different approaches. For this reason there are nine different diagrams types of UML. These diagrams are:

- Class Diagram,
- Object Diagram,
- State chart Diagram,
- Activity Diagram,
- Sequence Diagram,
- Collaboration Diagram,
- Use Case Diagram,
- Component Diagram,
- Deployment Diagram.

In business process modeling the best applicable diagrams are Use Case, Activity and Class Diagrams, but also State, Sequence and Collaboration diagrams can be very useful [HEMP 98]. The kind of diagrams that is being used in order to model a business process are the activity diagrams and they will be further analyzed and presented.

3.6.1 UML Activity Diagrams

Activity diagrams describe the way activities are coordinated. For example, an activity diagram may be used in order how an operation could be implemented. An activity diagram is very useful when we know that an organization has to achieve a number of different things and we want to model the essential dependencies between them. Thus, activity diagrams record these dependencies, which are the things that can happen in parallel and what must be finished before something else can start. As the name suggests, in activity diagrams the fundamental block is an activity, and a transition out of an activity normally means that the activity has been finished.

3.6.2 Elements of activity diagrams

The activity diagrams are constructed from six basic elements, the activity, the transition, the synchronization bar, the decision diamond, the start and the end marker [PSRP 00]:

- **Activity:** Is shown as a named box with a flat top and bottom and rounded sides. Technically this is a sort of state that is left, not in response to some event arriving from outside, but when the activity it represents is finished. The activity can involve many steps, including waiting for events, though this detailed activity is not usually shown.
- **Transition:** Is shown as an arrow. Transitions in an activity diagram are normally not labeled, because the transitions are caused by the completion of the previous

activity (rather than any kind of event) and it is normally more convenient to include actions in the activities rather than putting them separately on the transitions. However, there can be several outgoing transitions each with a guard, if the next activity depends on the situation.

- **Synchronization Bar**: Is shown as a thick horizontal bar describing the coordination of activities. Once all the activities that have transitions leading into the synchronization bar are complete, the bar can be passed. At that point, all the transitions leading out of the bar are fired, so the activities to which those transitions lead are started in parallel. The synchronization bar provides a way to express things like waiting for all subtasks to finish before proceeding (join) and starting several subtasks in parallel (fork).
- **Decision Diamond**: Is shown as a diamond and is used to represent decisions that must be taken, as an alternative to guards on separate transitions leaving the same state.
- **Start Marker**: Is shown as a black blob with an (unlabeled) arrow and means the start of the whole process.
- **Stop Marker**: Is shown as a black blob with a ring round it and means that the object has reached the end of its life.

In Figure 3.6 is shown the graphical representation of the basic elements that are mentioned above.

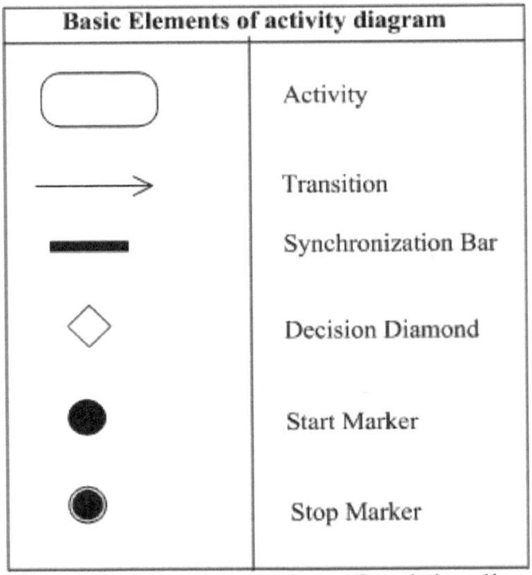

Figure 3.6: Graphical representation of activity diagram's basic elements

3.6.3 Examples of UML activity diagrams

The process behavior and the actions can be shown wit activity diagrams. An activity diagram is similar to flowcharts used in many modeling approaches. Furthermore the activity diagram supports powerful additions for dividing responsibilities and for showing parallel actions and changes of the states of objects. An activity diagram is very powerful in presenting processes, which go through different divisions of the organization [HSTJPO 02]. Activity diagrams show the general process and pathways at a high level.

In order to understand how activity diagrams are implemented and what kind of information is depicted from them, in the following are presented two examples. Figure 3.7 shows the activity diagram of the elevator while Figure 3.8 shows the activity diagram of the Library example.

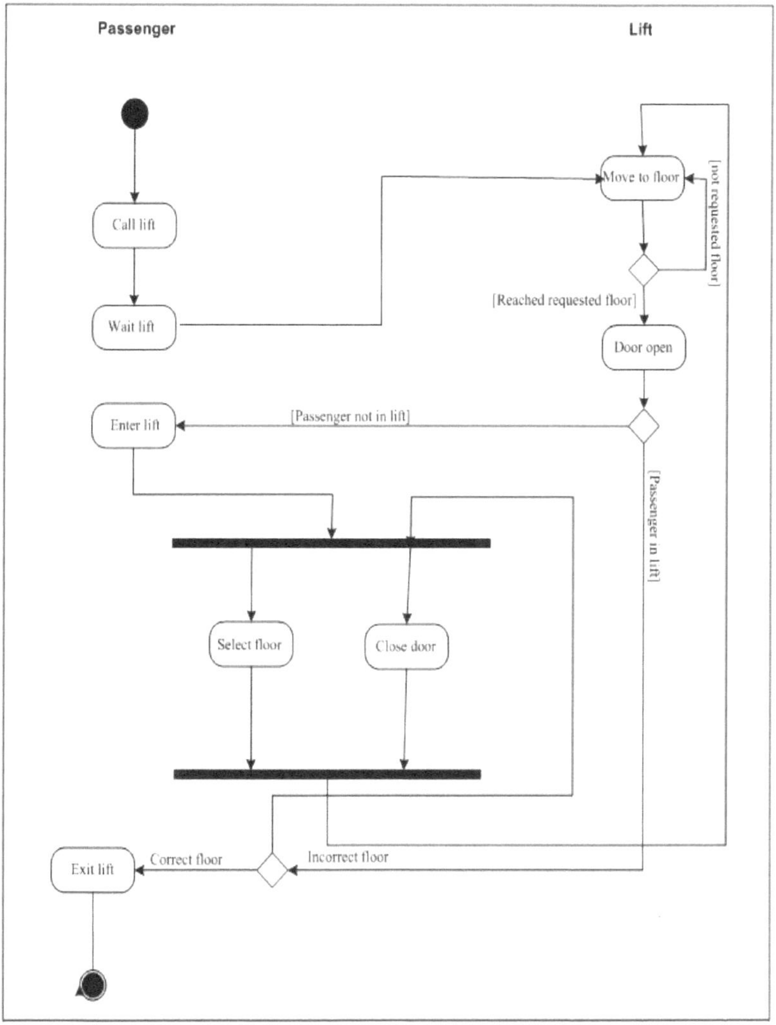

Figure 3.7: Activity diagram of the Elevator

The above activity diagram is analyzed as follows:

The participants of the whole process are two, the passenger and the lift and they are depicted in the topside of the diagram. The black blob indicates the starting point of the whole procedure. The first participant is the passenger. He calls the lift and it to arrive. After that he pushes the button in the lift in order to move to the floor that he wants. If he pushes the right button the lift's door opens, other wise he pushes the button in order to go the floor that he likes (decision diamond).

Then the passenger goes out of the lift. If he is in the correct floor the process ends, otherwise he enters the lift again in order to achieve his goal, which is to go to the floor that he wants. He enters the lift and two activities happen in parallel (Synchronization bar). He closes the door and selects the floor. Next the lift goes to the selected floor. If it is the correct floor the door opens. If it is the correct one the process stops (black blob with a ring around), otherwise the activities that are mentioned above take place in order the goal to be succeeded. Figure 3.8 that follow, represent a process that is too familiar to us. What is happening when we borrow or return a book in a library?

The participants in this process are two. The member and the librarian and they are represented in the diagram on the topside. The decision diamond shows whatever the member wants to borrow or to return a book to the librarian. If the member wants to borrow a book he goes to the self where he founds the one that he wants and after that he goes to the queue in order to be served. If he wants to return a borrowed book he goes to the queue too.

The activities that take place on behalf of the librarian depend on his needs that are borrowing or return a book. In the case of borrowing, the librarian gives the record borrowing and then prepare for next number and the process stops. In case of returning a book, the librarian gives the record of the return, puts the book on the right self, prepares for the next number and the process ends (black blob with a ring around).

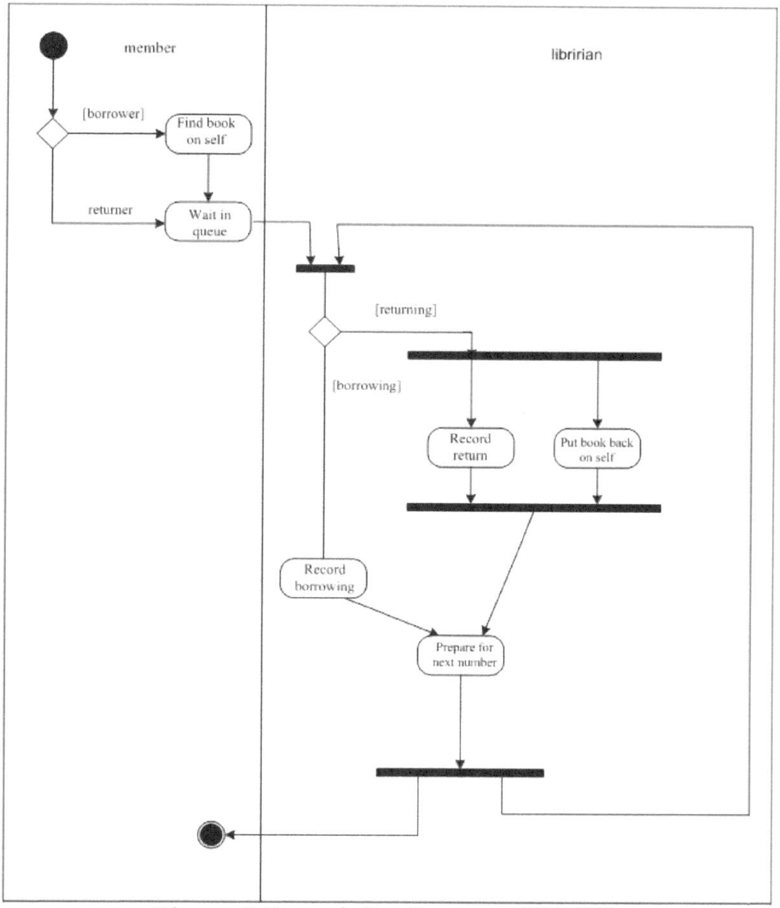

Figure 3.8: Activity diagram of the Library

3.6.4 Summarization

Although the proponents of UML themselves suggest that activity diagrams can be used for business process modeling [OMG 00] there is some doubt as to whether they actually cover all aspects required for modeling business processes. We use activity diagrams when:

- Activity diagrams show behavior that spans over multiple use cases to describe the workflow of the overall process.
- For multiple objects and their high-level interaction, activity diagrams are particularly helpful for representing an overview of concurrent processes.

We do not use activity diagrams when:

- To see how objects collaborate. An interaction diagram is simpler and gives you a clearer picture of collaborations.
- To describe how an object behaves over its lifetime. Activity diagrams in that case are not so accurate. State diagrams must be used instead.

4

EPC MODEL

4.1 INTRODUCTION

The SAP AG (www.sap.com), a leading provider of enterprise software solutions, has developed the R/3 reference model, which is a business process model for the processes supported by the R/3 enterprise software. The SAP R/3 reference model is primarily intended for identifying possibilities for "optimizing" the routines and procedures in a company. The most important addition to the R/3 model is the control logic – "when something should be done and in what order." Process descriptions are captured using *Event Driven Process Chains* (EPCs). The Event-Driven Process Chain Model (EPC Model) is a widely known and used notation for the description of business processes. In fact, it is an advanced form of flow chart diagrams.

EPCs are made up of active components that do things (functions) and passive components (inputs, outputs, organizational units, etc.) that only come into play in response to certain business situations. The events act as triggers for the functions. Identifying events in a process is not an easy task, but once they are identified, the resulting EPC acts as a control-flow logic diagram for the organization. A complex business process can be defined by connecting events with the functions using logical operators. The focus of the R/3 reference model is complete chains of processes in response to business events. In addition to describing the control flow, an EPC diagram has constructs to show the information/data necessary towards the development of an information system. Departments involved in carrying out the various functions in a process chain are also shown in the EPC diagram. The process selection matrix facilitates process modeling by providing the user with standard business processes and their scenarios [MKNDACESWK 03].

4.2 EPC NOTATION

EPC has a very easy to understand notation. This is the main strength of EPC method. Its notation is capable of representing business information systems while at the same time other important features such as functions, data, organizational structure and informational resources. This makes as a result the acceptance of EPC as a widely standard to denote business processes.

In Figure 4.1 are shown the elements that are being used in order to construct the EPC model. In the following is presented a description of these elements [Fer 01]:

- **Event:** The events are passive elements in EPC. They describe under what circumstances a function or a process works, or which state a function or a process results. Examples of events are "Material on Stock". In an EPC diagram, an event is represented as a hexagon.
- **Function:** In EPC functions are active elements. They model the tasks or activities within the organization. Functions describe transformations from an initial state to a resulting state. In case different resulting states can occur, the selection of the respective resulting state can be modeled explicitly as a decision function using logical connectors. Functions can be refined into another EPC diagram. In this situation it is called hierarchical function. Examples of functions are "Check Material on Stock", "Capture Requirement",

e.t.c. In the EPC diagram, the function is represented as a rounded rectangle.

- **Information, Material or Resource Object:** The information, material or resource object in the EPC diagram, represent objects in the real world such as entities, business objects, e.t.c., which can be input data serving as the basis for a function, or output data produced by a function. Examples are “Order”, “Material”, e.t.c. In the EPC diagram (graph) such an object is represented as a rectangle.
- **Organization Unit:** The organization units determine which person or which organization within the structure of an enterprise is responsible for a specific function. Examples are “ Sales Manager”, “Sales Department”, “Procurement Manager”, and e.t.c. In the EPC graph is represented as an ellipse with a vertical line.
- **Process Path:** The process paths serve as navigation aid in the EPC diagram. They depict (show) the connection from or to other process. In figure 4.2 is shown the use of process paths. There are two EPCs – process 1 and process 2. We can show the continuation from the process 1 to process 2 with a process path at the end of process 1 pointing to process 2 and in the beginning of process 2 referring to process 1. A process path in an EPC graph is represented as a “function and event” symbol (the function symbol in front of the event symbol).
- **Control Flow:** A flow control connects the events with functions, process paths, logical connectors creating chronological sequences and logical independencies between them. A control flow is presented as a dashed arrow in an EPC graph.
- **Information Flow:** The information flow shows the connection between functions and input or output data, upon which function reads, writes or changes.

- **Organization Unit Assignment**: The organization unit assignments show the connection between an organization unit and the function that it is responsible for.
- **Logical Connector:** The logical connectors in the EPC describe the logical connections between elements in the control flow, that is, events and functions. Logical connectors are very helpful because by using them it is possible to split the control flow from one flow to two or more flows and to synchronize the control flow from two or more flows to one flow. There are three kind of logical relationships defined in EPC. The Branch/Merge, the Fork/Join, and the OR relationship.

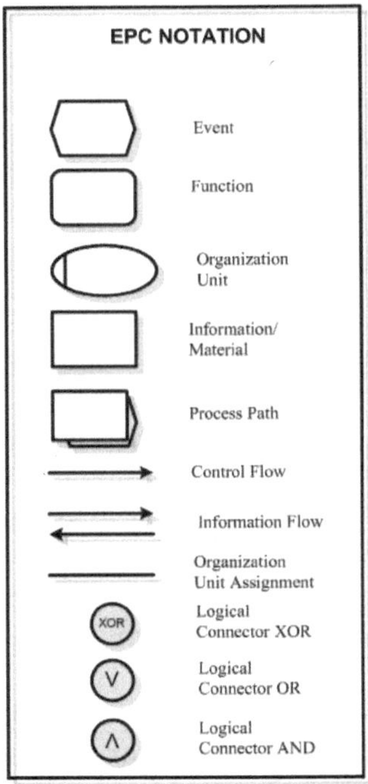

Figure 4.1: Elements used in EPC diagram

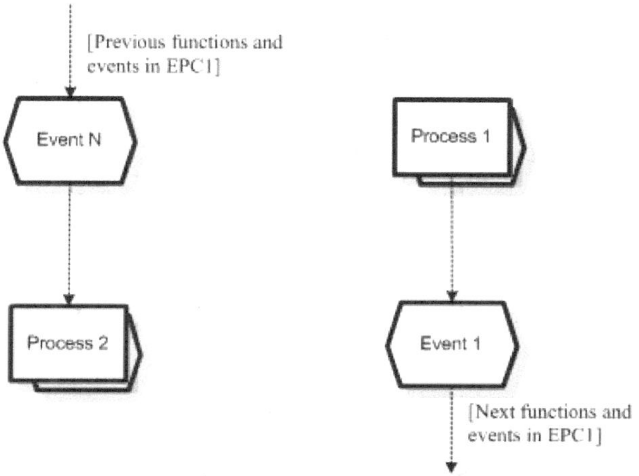

Figure 4.2: Process Paths to show connection from EPC1 to EPC2

In the following a description of the logical connectors is presented:

- **Branch/Merge**: Branch and merge correspond to making decision of which path to choose among several control flows. A branch may have one incoming control flow and two or more outgoing control flows. When the condition is fulfilled a branch activates exactly only one of the outgoing control flows and deactivates the other control flows. The counterpart of the branch is the merge. A merge may have two or more incoming control flows and one outgoing control flow. It synchronizes an activated and the deactivated alternatives. The control will then be passed to the next element after the merge. A branch in the EPC diagram is represented by an opening "XOR", and a merge is represented as a closing "XOR" connectors, as we can see in Figure 4.3.

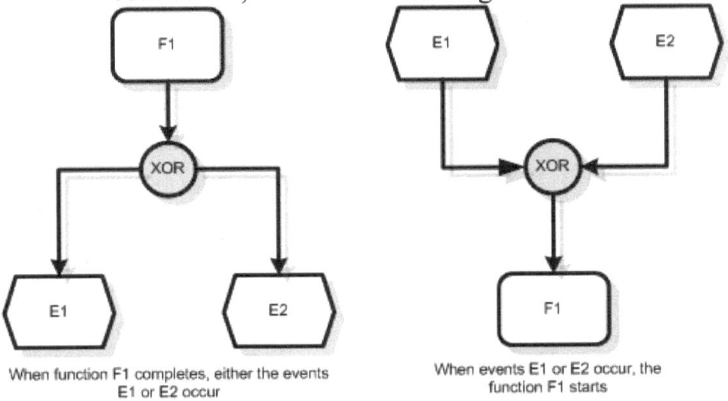

Figure 4.3: Branch and Merge

- **Fork/Join**: These two elements correspond to activating all paths in the control flow concurrently. A fork may have one incoming control flow and two or more outgoing control flows. When the condition is fulfilled a fork activates all of the outgoing control flows in parallel. A join may have two or more incoming control flows and only one outgoing control flow. It makes the synchronization of all the activated incoming control flows. In the EPC diagram is not a matter the way the concurrency is achieved. In real world the concurrency can be achieved by the true parallelism or by virtual concurrency achieved by interleaving. A fork is represented by an opening "AND" and a join in an EPC diagram is represented as a closing "AND" connector, as we can see in Figure 4.4.

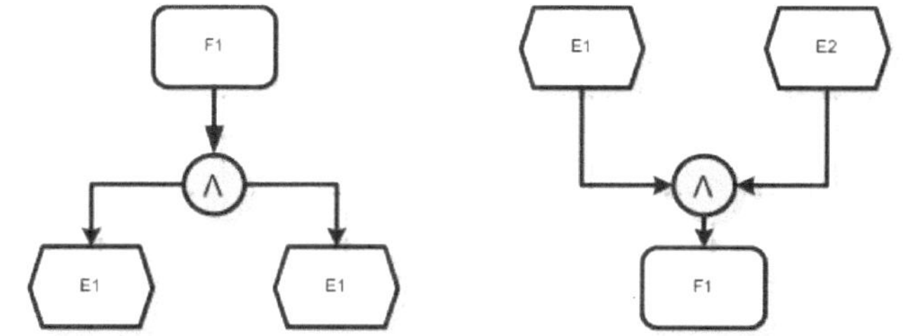

When function F1 completes both the events E1 and E2 occur

When both the events E1 or E2 occur, the function F1 starts

Figure 4.4: Fork and Join

- **"OR"**: An OR relationship corresponds to activating one or more paths among control flows. An opening "OR" logical connector may have one incoming control flow and two or more outgoing control flows. When the condition is fulfilled an opening "OR" connector activates one or more control flows and deactivates the rest of them. The counterpart of this is the closing "OR" logical connector. When at least one of the incoming control flows is activated, the closing "OR" connector will pass the control to the next element after it, as we can see in Figure 4.5 that follows.
-

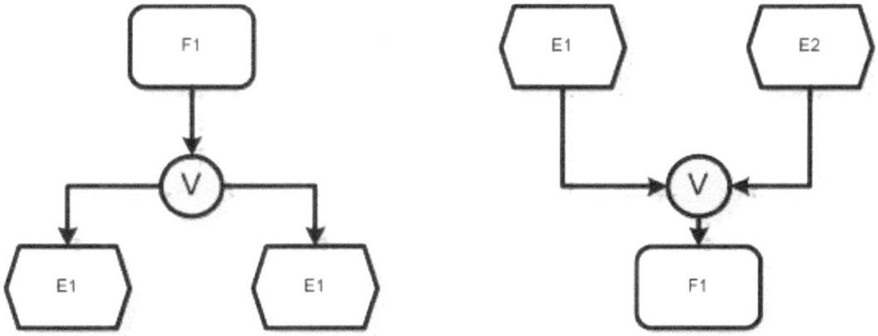

When function F1 completes, the events E1 or E2 occur

When either the events E1 or E2 or both occur, the function F1 starts

Figure 4.5: Inclusive OR connectors

4.3 EPC NOTATION RULES

In the previous section the EPC notation was depicted. In the current section some aspects and hints will be given in order to create an EPC diagram properly. A function in an EPC diagram has always a following event, while an event can only be followed by a function. In a single EPC graph without process paths, the path must have at least one start event and one end event. In other words a graph must be started and ended with events and not with functions.

An event is always a passive element. This means that it cannot be used to make decisions but it can be used to trigger parallel activities. Therefore an event can be followed only by an "AND" logical connector and not by an "OR" or "XOR" logical connectors, as we can see in Figure 4.6 that follows.

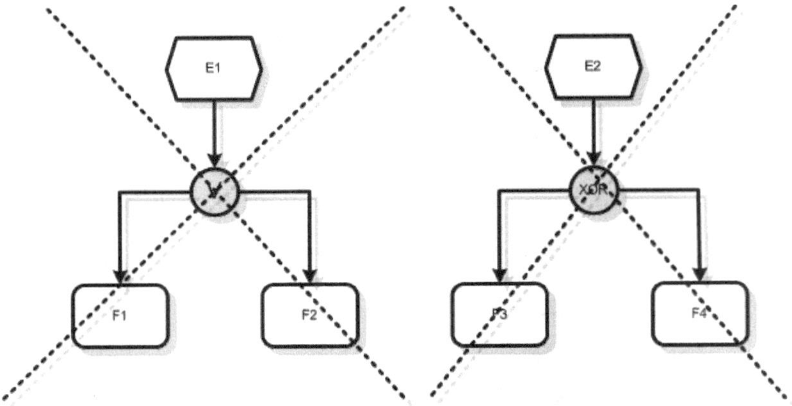

Figure 4.6: Connections in EPC that are not allowed

In case that the EPC graphs have process paths that link them, in the source graph the process path should be put at the end of the graph after the end event, and in the target graph the process path should be put at the beginning of the graph before the start event. A combination of functions and events can be achieved by using logical connectors. The logical connectors can be placed between functions on the one hand and events on the other hand, but the alternation of functions and events must always be maintained. A function is an active element so it can be used to make decisions and to trigger parallel activities. Therefore any of the logical connectors can follow a function.

The logical connectors should match. This means that an opening "XOR" logical connector serving as a branch should be closed by another "XOR" connector. The same rule applies and to fork/join by using "AND" connector and "OR" connector. Last but not least all the elements must be connected to the control flow, because an non connected element would have no meaning or contribution to the whole process that is being modeled [Fer 01].In Figure 4.7 is by [ESBAPJEPBW 02] is shown an example of an EPC diagram.

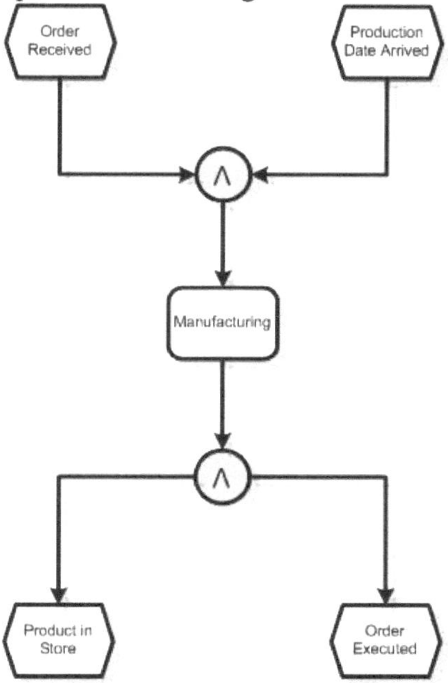

Figure 4.7: Example of EPC

In Figure 4.7 the EPC diagram shows that two events, *Order Received* and *Production Date Arrived* must occur before the business function *Manufacturing* can take place. When the function is completed, two additional events must occur: *Product in Store* and *Order Executed.* In Figure 4.8 that follows, is shown the general structure of an EPC diagram [MNTFVZ 98].

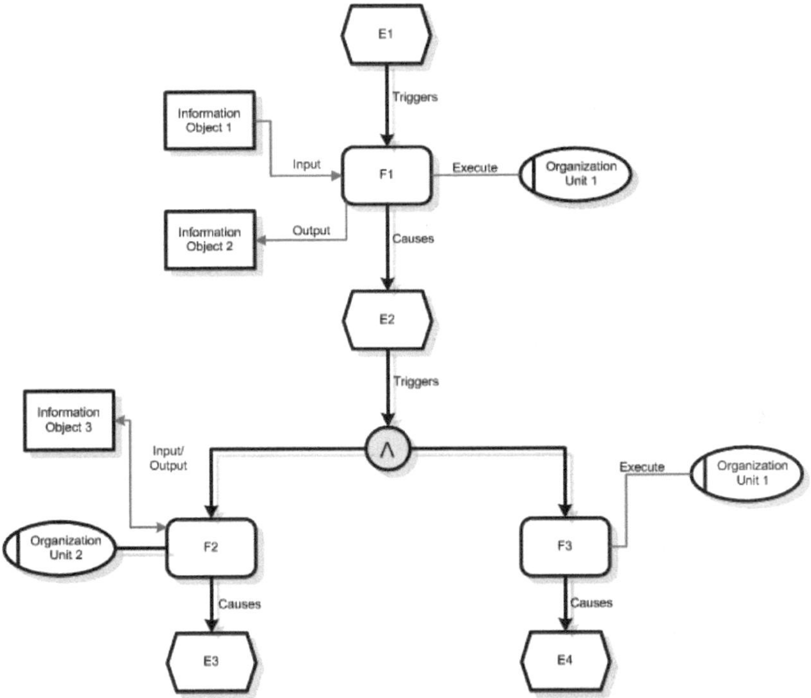

Figure 4.8: EPC diagram in general

4.4 SUMMARIZATION OF EPC METHOD

EPCs can be hierarchically structured across any number of levels by assigning more detailed EPCs to every function within an EPC. Such a detailed EPC denotes the process, which is carried out when the respective function is triggered. Functions, for which it is not feasible to define an even more detailed process, are called "elementary functions". Events can also be described with so-called event-diagrams, in which a complex event (such as "order checked") is decomposed into detailed events (such as "customer data checked" and "product data checked"). An event can be connected to data view elements, such as attributes, so that it is possible to model the fact that an event occurs when both the preceding function is finished and a specific attribute has a certain value. An event can also be directly related to a product, if the event just describes the occurrence of a function's output [TAPL 98].

In addition to functions, events, data objects, products, and organizational elements, a wide range of information can be included into an EPC in order to describe specific aspects more clearly. Such types of information include:

- The use of different kinds of information carriers and communication media, such as paper documents, floppy disks, telephone etc.,
- Information systems used for supporting functions,
- Human know-how and qualifications,
- In- and output material of a function (e.g. in the production),
- Required equipment or machinery (resources).

In many cases, there can be different types of connections between two kinds of elements. Between an organizational unit and a function, for example, there can be several connection types, such as:

- Organizational unit *carries out* function
- Organizational unit *is responsible for* function
- Organizational unit *provides support for* function
- Organizational unit *must be informed about* function
- Organizational unit *must approve of* function

These different kinds of connections can be used for modeling in detail how different organizational units work together in order to perform the functions of a process. Only a part of the information about a business process is shown in the EPC diagram, because each element and each connector possesses various characteristics, which are expressed through attributes. There are general attributes, which are common to all types of elements, such as the identifier or the description, but most of the attributes are type-specific, e. g. for a function there are attributes concerning the time (such as the minimum, the maximum and the average times for processing, waiting, and transfer) and costs. Connectors can also have attributes, such as probabilities for control flow connectors. Not all of the rich semantics can and should be used within a single project. The types of elements, connectors and attributes to be used depend on the modeling purpose. In an EPC, which should be simulated, it is necessary to define probabilities and resource capacities, while for a workflow EPC it is important to assign people and roles to the functions [PLTA 98].

One of the main advantages of the EPC is that it is both powerful and easily understandable for end-users. EPCs are often used for capturing and discussing business processes with people who have never been trained in any kind of modeling technique, e. g. with workers on the shop floor. Although EPCs can be understood even by a short-time trained personnel, the same models can be refined and used for the requirements definition of an information system. This is one of the reasons that both many end-user companies and many software vendors are using EPCs for business process modeling [PLPF 00].

A distinguishing feature of the EPC diagram is the explicit modeling of events. This becomes important because one of the main functions of the EPC diagram is to specify the transaction processing logic within SAP's ERP system in response to business events. [MKNDACESWK 03].

Despite its popularity, EPC has some drawbacks mainly because the initial goal of its use is to create a simple documentation of business processes. Documenting a business process does not require either a formal syntax or formal semantics. Therefore, EPC lacks formal syntax and well-defined semantics, which are essential elements for model simulation and enactment. Furthermore, EPC model does not offer a possibility to specify in more detail the data flow, the conditions of the control flow and the functions - activities of a business process.

5

COMPARISON OF THE MODELS - CONCLUSIONS

5.1 THE REPRESENTED MODELS

IDEF (Integrated Definition) diagrams were introduced in 1981 as a part of the ICAM (Computer-Aided Manufacturing) project. There are numerous IDEF methods but two of them serve as the basis of business process modelling: the IDEF0 and the IDEF3 method. The IDEF0 method focuses on activity modelling and IDEF3 method accomplishes process desc82ription and can be used to generate simulation model specifications [[RMPBBCMP 98], [LWBHAP 97]].

IDEF0

IDEF0 method is a technique that produces a function model of a new or existing system or a subject area and results the IDEF0 model of the system. IDEF0 uses one notational construct called ICOM (Input – Control – Output – Mechanism). The elements of IDEF0 are boxes and arrows. The activity (or function) is represented by boxes; inputs are represented by the arrows flowing into the left hand side of an activity box; outputs are represented by arrows flowing out the right hand side of an activity box; the arrows flowing into the top portion of the box represent constraints or controls on the activities; and the final element represented by arrows flowing into the bottom of the activity box are the mechanisms that carry out the activity

Perhaps the main strength of IDEF0 is its simplicity, as it uses – as we mentioned above – only one notational construct, called the ICOM (Input – Control – Output – Mechanism) So using the IDEF0 method we model activities, decisions, and actions of an organization or a system, targeted upon the functional perspective of the system. One characteristic of the IDEF0 modelling technique is that each activity and the arrows can be decomposed (or exploded) into more detailed level of analysis. This characteristic is especially useful in enterprise (organization), modelling where details about lower level activities can be captured, but at the same time, be hidden from models of the organization at higher more abstract levels.

IDEF3

IDEF3 is not intended to be a replacement for IDEF0. We can say that IDEF3 is a technique used to produce a dynamic model of the system, as it can produce two views of the system; a process-centred view and an object-centred view [CBMBCF 02]. IDEF3 describes processes, as ordered sequences of events or activities. As such, IDEF3 is a scenario-driven process flow modelling technique, which is based on the direct capture of precedence and causality relations between situations and events [RMPBBCMP 98]. The goal of an IDEF3 model is to provide a structured method for expressing the domain expert's knowledge about how a particular system or organization works (as opposed to IDEF0, which is mainly concerned with what activities the organization performs) [VVGGVH 03].

Similar to IDEF0 method, the main strength of IDEF3 is the simplicity of its notation, which relies on its basic construct, which is called the UOB (Unit of Behaviour). The Units of Behaviours represent types of happenings (such as events, acts, and e.t.c.) and describes the actual detailed in the box. The other basic elements of IDEF3 are Junctions and Links. Links connect the boxes and describe the relationships between the various UOBs. Junctions explicitly describe the logic of multiple links either coming together or spreading apart. The IDEF3 method does not explicitly limit the number of activities which can exist within a given process model [LWBHAP 97]. This means that a process could be represented within one level of abstraction using the IDEF3 method, while using the IDEF0 technique, multiple decompositions of the system model are required.

IDEF3 integrates very well with IDEF0. The IDEF0 method can be used to build high level models of business process by abstracting away from timing, sequencing and decision logic. The IDEF3 method takes the knowledge captured in IDEF0, supplements it with a process owner's real-world knowledge of how a process works, and produces accurate process scenarios [May at al 95]. These scenarios can be used to see in detail the process under study. Due to the method's formal semantics and syntax, the produced scenarios can feed directly into simulation scenarios. This means that a process could be represented within one level of abstraction using the IDEF3 method, while using the IDEF0 technique, multiple decompositions of the system model are usually required.

UML Activity Diagrams

Activity Diagrams describe how activities are coordinated. They record the dependencies between activities, such as which things can happen in parallel and what must be finished before something else can start. As a result the fundamental block in activity diagram is an activity, and a transition out of an activity means that the activity has been completed (in most cases).

The basic elements of the activity diagrams are activities, transitions, synchronization bar, decision diamond start and stop markers. To be more precise according to [PSRP 00] is shown as a named box with rounded corners. The activity can involve many steps including waiting for events. The transitions are shown as arrows because the transitions are caused by the completion of the previous activity. The synchronization bar describes the coordination of the activities. It provides the way to express the join (all subtask must finish in order to proceed) and fork (several subtasks start in parallel). The decision diamond is used to show the decisions that might be taken and finally the start and the end markers are used in order to show the start or the finish of the represented process respectively.

The activity diagram is used to describe how things are done, the work that is performed. Activity diagrams can be used for operations, classes, or use cases, but they may also used to show the workflow. Activity diagrams can be used to model organizations. Using activity diagrams has similarities to implementing techniques such as IDEF0. The approach to modelling business with activity diagrams may be complemented with use cases or other techniques to capture the requirements of the business system [HEMP 98].

EPC (Event-Driven Process Chain)

The basic elements of the EPC model are: Event, Function, Information Object, Control Flow, Process Paths, Organization Unit, and Logical Connectors. The event reflects a signal in a business environment, which triggers the execution of a function. A function is a (business) activity that is executed either by a person or automatically. After the execution of a function an event is produced. The information objects describe what information is needed for the execution of an activity (function inputs) and what information is produced by an activity (function output). Functions can be connected to an organizational unit to define responsibility for the execution of the activity. Process paths are connections to other EPCs to divide business processes into various EPCs. The logical connectors are used to describe the logic of control flow.

One of the main advantages of the EPC is that it is both powerful and easily understandable for end-users. EPCs are often used for capturing and discussing business processes with people who have never been trained in any kind of modeling technique, e. g. with workers on the shop floor. Although EPCs can be understood even by a short-time trained personnel, the same models can be refined and used for the requirements definition of an information system. This is one of the reasons that both many end-user companies and many software vendors are using EPCs for business process modeling [PLPF 00].

A distinguishing feature of the EPC diagram is the explicit modeling of events. This becomes important because one of the main functions of the EPC diagram is to specify the transaction processing logic within SAP's ERP system in response to business events. [MKNDACESWK 03].

EPC has some drawbacks mainly because the initial goal of its use is to create a simple documentation of business processes. Documenting a business process does not require either a formal syntax or formal semantics. Therefore, EPC lacks formal syntax and well-defined semantics, which are essential elements for model simulation and enactment. Furthermore, EPC model does not offer a possibility to specify in more detail the data flow, the conditions of the control flow and the functions - activities of a business process.

5.2 PROCESS MODELING: A CASE STUDY

The following Purchasing System example adopted by [MKNDACESWK 03] is used to illustrate the process modeling features of the enterprise modeling efforts that were analyzed in the previous chapters. When a material request arrives from Material Planning the purchasing system prepares a purchase order and sends it to the supplier. A copy of the purchase order is stored in a shared database. If the material received matches the purchase order completely, then Receiving accepts it and adds a receipt confirmation to the shared database. When an invoice arrives, Accounts Payable uses the purchase order to verify that the material was ordered and the receipt

confirmation to verify that the supplier delivered it before making the payment.
In Figure 5.1 is shown the IDEF0 representation of the above problem.

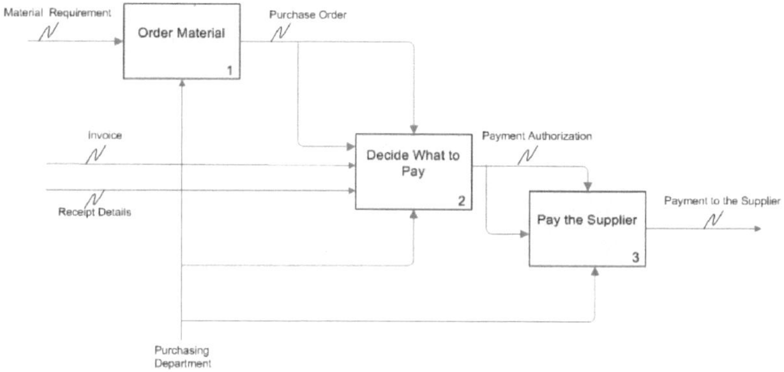

Figure 5.1: IDEF0 diagram of the Purchasing System

As we can see in the above Figure an output from one activity (box) can be an input to another activity and the arrows depict the sequence of them. The activity *Order material*, has as an input the *Material requirement* and the mechanisms needed to be established is the *Purchasing Department*. This results the *Purchase Order*, which is an input as well as a control to the activity *Decide What to Pay*. This activity has as inputs, except the *Purchase Order*, the *Invoice* and the *Receipt Details*. These happen to the *Purchasing Department* and results the *Payment authorization*. The *Payment authorization* is an input as well as a control to the activity *Pay the supplier*. This activity is happening in the *Purchasing department* and has as a result the *Payment to the supplier*.
In Figure 5.2 is shown the IDEF3 representation of the Purchasing system.

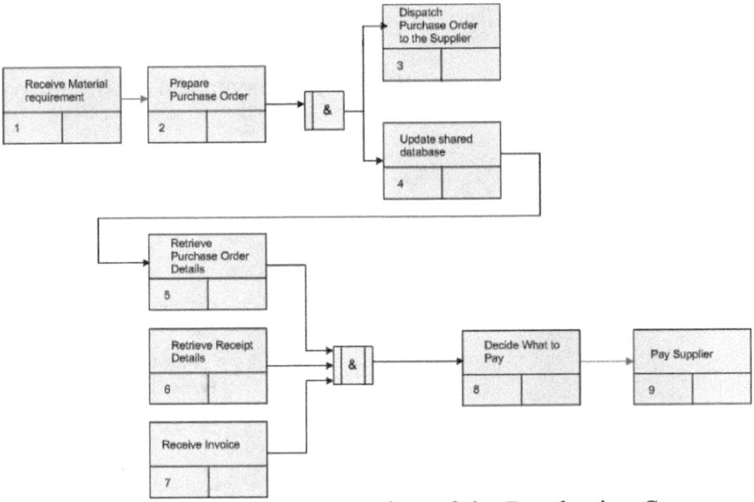

Figure 5.2: IDEF3 representation of the Purchasing System

In the IDEF3 process description diagram, each activity is represented by rectangle termed a Unit of Behavior (UOB). The arcs represent the control flow and connect the UOBs and as a result depict the process sequence. The junctions describe the logic (AND, XOR, etc.) of multiple arcs. According to Figure 5.2 when the *Material requirement* is received the *Purchase Order* can be prepared. Furthermore, when the *Purchase Order Details*, the *Receipt Details* are retrieved and the *Invoice* is received (all these joined by Synchronous AND) the decision *What to Pay* can be made. After that the *Supplier* can be *Paid.*

In Figure 5.3 is shown the UML activity diagram of the Purchasing system.

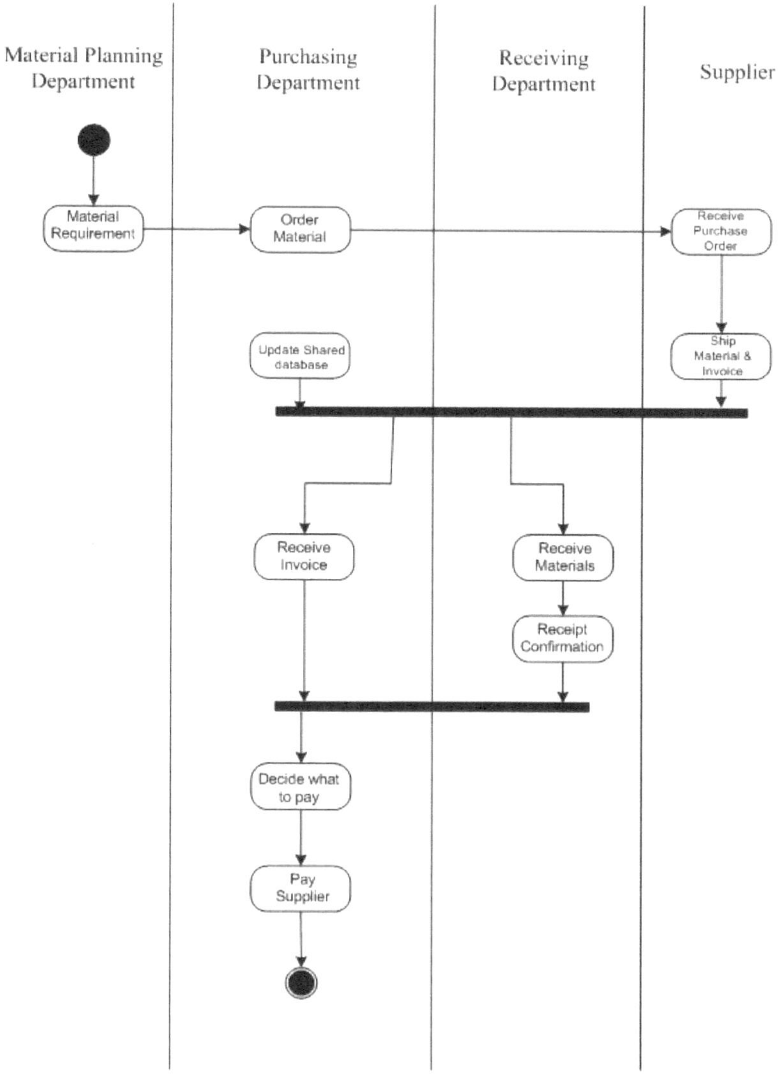

Figure 5.3: UML activity diagram of the Purchasing System

The basic element in the UML activity diagram is the *activity*. Using a UML activity diagram we can graphically depict the control flow through activities of a business process. The emphasis on these diagrams is on depicting the control flow. The participants in the whole procedure are the *Material Planning Department*, the *Purchasing Department*, the *Receiving Department* and the *Supplier* and they are depicted on the topside of the activity diagram. The starting as well as the stop point is represented. Every participant follows its own activities. These activities can be made and in parallel. When one activity completes, another activity takes place. The arc shows the completion of the activity.

The EPC diagram is activities of active and passive elements. The active elements are the *functions* (make things) and they are presented as rounded rectangles. The passive elements are the *inputs*, *outputs*, *organization units* and come into play only in response to certain business situations. The *events* (represented by hexagons) act as triggers for the functions. In the above figure (Figure 5.4) we can see that the activities (functions) are three: the *Order Material*, the *Decide What to Pay* and *Pay the Supplier*. Every function is triggered by an event (etc. *Payment authorized*), has data elements as inputs or outputs (etc. *Receipt details* or *Payment authorization*). What is input or output can be recognized by the data flow orientation. All these take place into an organization unit (*Purchasing Department*).

In Figure 5.4 is shown the EPC representation of the Purchasing System:

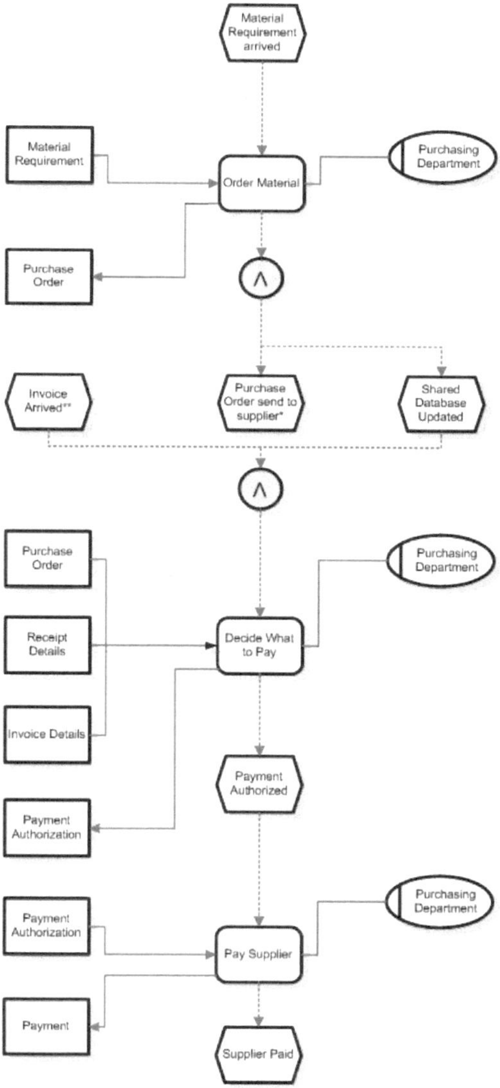

* Triggers event at Suppliers end
** External event specifying arrival or invoice from Supplier

Figure 5.4: EPC model of the Purchasing System

5.3 COMPARISON OF THE MODELS - CONCLUSIONS

In the previous chapters four different models were presented and analyzed. In this section we will compare the above models according to some criteria in order to find the most suitable model for us. The comparison of business process modeling techniques is a very potential issue, because there are many business process modeling techniques (not only these presented to the current thesis) and some how there must be a distinguish between them. Many researchers were focused on the comparison of the different process modeling approaches such as [[Nor 03], [HMGJELGTAP], [JDRY 00], [TAPL 98], [PLTA 98], [MNTFVZ 98], [Gia 01], [MKNDACESWK 03], [Tsa 02], [ESBAPJEPBW 02], [VVGGVH 03]].

The models that were analyzed in the previous chapters and presented for the case study of the Purchasing System (Figure 5.1 up to Figure 5.4) now are being compared according to different kind of criteria in order to find their applicability for business process modeling.

According to [Tsa 02] and [VVGGVH 03] there are some criteria in order to examine the applicability of a selected model, and these criteria are:

- *Simplicity*: How easily a process can be modeled by the selected model, and how easy (simple) the basic principles (elements) of the model can be understood,
- *Hierarchical Decomposition*: If the model enables decomposition of the process model and the construction of model hierarchies,
- *Originality*: If the model was developed for business process modeling or for other reason,
- *Comprehensibility*: If the process model enhances the process participants to understand the process and enables the communication between them,

- *Expressiveness*: If the relationships between the activities of the process can be represented and iteration, time relationships, conditions selection can be expressed by the model,
- *Formal Syntax and Semantics*: If the model has a well defined semantics and a formal syntax.
- *Standardization of the models,*
- *Software that supports the methods.*

According to the above criteria (features) the comparison of the models described in Table 5.1:

Table 5.1: Basic Features of the models

FEATURES OF THE MODELS				
FEATURE	**IDEF0**	**IDEF3**	**EPC**	**UML Activity Diagram**
Simplicity	High	Medium	High	High
Hierarchical Decomposition	Yes	No	No	No
Originality	No	Yes	Yes	No
Comprehensibility	Very good	Good	Good	Good
Expressiveness	No	Yes	Yes	Yes
Formal Syntax and Semantics	No	Yes	No	No
Standardization	Yes	Yes	Yes	Yes
Software	Numerous	Numerous	Numerous	Numerous

The IDEF0 diagrams as well as the UML activity diagrams and EPC diagrams are very easy to use while IDEF3 is not so easy. Only the IDEF0 diagram gives the opportunity of hierarchical decomposition of the activities since as mentioned to other chapters an activity (box) can be decomposed to other activities. IDEF0 and UML activity diagrams do not provide originality as they where made not exactly for business modeling issues. The IDEF0 is coming from the manufacturing section and UML activity diagrams come from the software development section. There are numerous software tools for all the mentioned methods (such as Visio, SmartDraw, etc.). IDEF0 model show what is happening (activities, entities, resources, controls). The IDEF3 diagrams show how this is happening (by junctions, relational links). The UML activity diagram is used to describe how things are done, the work that is performed. The EPC diagrams specify the transaction processing logic in response to business events.

A very critical topic (term) for the applicability of a modeling technique is the term *expressiveness*. As we can see from Table 5.1, IDEF0 technique does not provide expressiveness. This happens because IDEF0 diagrams cannot derive the logical sequence of activities. A branching of an arrow as we can see in Figure 5.1, into one or more arrows does not mean a logical branching but the fact that an arrow can split in to two or more paths that are inputs or controls to other boxes (activities). Moreover IDEF0 diagrams lack of time dependency and as a result we can say that they have a restriction on the use. IDEF3 satisfies the term expressiveness. In IDEF3 diagrams the arrows connecting the boxes indicate the relationships between the processes. The junctions indicate the different conditions in which an activity is carried out as if they were logical operators: AND, OR, XOR.

An EPC model; include information such as the people as well as the organizational units that are responsible to carry out a certain function as well as a data flow. In EPC models can be depicted which organization role carries out the function as we can see in Figure 5.4. There logical connectors that can give a path selection. So EPC models satisfy the term expressiveness.

An UML activity diagram, offer elements such as relationships for control flow, decisions, synchronization bar and these elements can be grouped to swimlanes. Thus UML activity diagrams satisfy the term expressiveness.

The process models can have different goals and as a result the modelers may have different needs from the models. According to [[Gia 01], [HMGJELGTAP]] a process model may have four different goals (views):

- *Functional View*: If the activities are being performed and the data dependencies between them,
- *Information View*: The objects produced by the process (etc. real world objects),
- *Organizational View*: The actors and roles that are responsible for executing the activities,
- *Behavioral or Dynamic View*: Sequencing, decision making, feedback, triggering condition.

Due to the above criteria (views) the comparison of the models is given in 5.2:

Table 5.2: Model views

Views of the models				
MODEL	**Informational View**	**Functional View**	**Organizational View**	**Dynamic or Behavioral View**
IDEF0	-	Yes	-	-
IDEF3	-	-	-	Yes
EPC	Yes	-	Yes	Yes
UML Activity Diagram	-	-	Yes	Yes

As we can see in Table 5.2, the IDEF0 covers only the Functional view. This happens because these kind of diagrams indicate the "what" but not the "how" (IDEF3 diagrams – that's why IDEF3 cover the Dynamic View). EPC models cover the Informational, Organizational and Behavioral views. In EPC it is possible to depict the products that can be produced by a process (information object), the actors that are responsible for the execution of the activity can be depicted (organizational unit) and lastly terms like decision-making and triggering conditions can be depicted. UML activity diagrams cover the Organizational and Dynamic View of the process. This happens because the participants can be depicted (swimlanes) and terms like decision-making, feedback etc. can be depicted.

The choice of the proper technique has a crucial impact on the effective enmodelation of the business process. A clear answer cannot always be given and it is depended on the kind of the process, the modeler's background, the existing resources and the goal of business process analysis.

According to our investigations (Table 5.1 and Table 5.2) EPC and UML techniques give a number of serious advantages for business process modeling. IDEF0 model has a strong restriction of use compared to the other models. Diagramming with IDEF3 does not require previous use of IDEF0, as IDEF0 captures the activities that are completed and IDEF3 captures the process flows that cannot be captured in IDEF3. Thus IDEF3 and IDEF0 can be used in complementally. When a process is very complex in order to be modeled by IDEF diagrams, it is better to make the IDEF0 diagram for the activity modeling and the IDEF3 diagram for the process flow description.

IDEF0 and IDEF3 diagrams can be used to support simulation of alternative process implementations because of their multiple views and the decomposition that they provide. EPC diagrams allow users to analyze business processes independent of organizational restriction since they focus on control flows. UML diagrams may not be appropriate for an enterprise user that is interesting in describing process details but on the other hand may be appropriate for an information system analyst who wants to develop software specifications based on the process details provided by an enterprise user.

Comparing EPC and UML activity diagram we can see many similarities as well as some differences between them, which are presented to Table 5.3:

Table 5.3: Comparison between EPC and UML activity diagram

Comparison EPC and UML Activity diagram		
Notation/Terminology	**EPC**	**UML Activity Diagram**
Active Element	Function	Activity
Passive Element	Event	-
Process Chain	Control Flow	Transition
Branch/Merge	XOR Connector	Decision Diamond
Fork/Join	AND Connector	Synchronization Bar
Inclusive OR	OR Connector	-
Start/End Point	-	Yes
Actor	Organization Unit	Swimlane

Table 5.3 gives a comparison between EPC and UML activity diagram against their notation. As we can see there are many similarities. First of all both models have an active element. The control flow in EPC corresponds to the Transition in the activity diagram. The "XOR" and "AND" connectors correspond to Decision Diamond and to Synchronization Bar respectively. As we can see their differences are pointed at the

casualty of the passive element and the "inclusive OR" in the UML activity diagrams.

In order to translate EPC diagrams to UML activity diagrams and vice versa we can follow some guidelines. First of all the organizational units that are involved in the process chain must be aligned into separate swimlanes in an activity diagram. Each function can be translated into activity/action states in the activity diagram. The produced action must be depicted in the swimlane of the organization unit that is responsible for it. The branches and merges represented by "XOR" connectors in the EPC are transformed into decision diamonds and the forks and joins ("AND" logical connectors) are transformed into synchronization bars. Then, according to the control flow in the EPC, the activities, the decision diamonds and the synchronization bars are connected. Lastly, the start and stop events must be depicted into the activity diagram.

Due to their differences, there are some problems during the translation. According to Table 5.3 the "OR" connector cannot be translated into the activity diagram. In order to achieve the "OR" connector the logical theory must be used. For two variables x and y we have: x or $y \Leftrightarrow (xxory)$ x or $(xandy)$. Using this equation of the logic theory, the "OR" connector can be translated into two alternative paths based on an opening and a closing connectors (Figure 5.5).
Into the reverse procedure we have:

The activity/action states from the activity diagrams are transformed into functions in the EPC. The decision diamonds and the synchronization bars are transformed into "XOR" and "AND" connectors. After and each function some events must be created that trigger or being produced by the functions. The produced elements (functions, events, connectors), are connected with control flow according to the transitions. The functions must be connected to the organizational units transformed from the swimlanes. The problems that might appear originate to the fact that events are elements that don't appear into activity diagrams. Furthermore activity diagrams do not contain information about material or information objects, so the resulting EPC diagram is not a complete one as it contains only the flows and the organizational units.

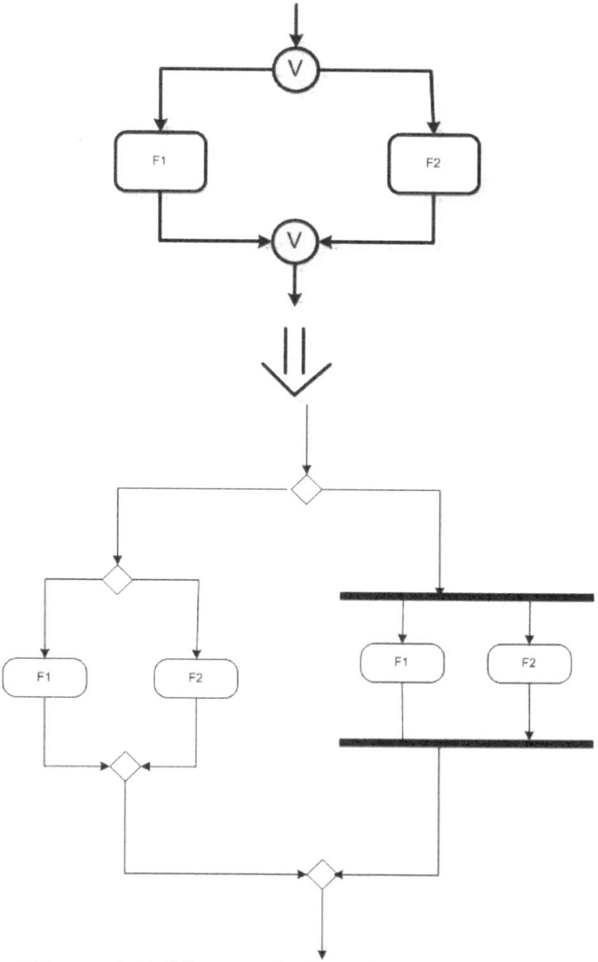

Figure 5.5: The translation of "OR" connector

Into the reverse procedure we have:

The activity/action states from the activity diagrams are transformed into functions in the EPC. The decision diamonds and the synchronization bars are transformed into "XOR" and "AND" connectors. After and each function some events must be created that trigger or being produced by the functions. The produced elements (functions, events, connectors), are connected with control flow according to the transitions. The functions must be connected to the organizational units transformed from the swimlanes. The problems that might appear originate to the fact that events are elements that don't appear into activity diagrams. Furthermore activity diagrams do not contain information about material or information objects, so the resulting EPC diagram is not a complete one as it contains only the flows and the organizational units.

Even EPC and UML activity diagrams were developed in different contexts have great similarities, so it is possible to translate EPC diagrams to UML activity diagrams and vice versa. The differences that exist between them have as a result loss of information when we translate from EPC to UML activity diagram and loss of details on the other way.

REFERENCES

BOOKS

[HEMP 98] Hans-Erik Ericsson, M. Penker, "UML Toolkit", John Wiley & Sons, New York, 1998

[PSRP 00] P. Stevens, R. Pooley, "Using UML: Software Engineering With Objects And Components", Addison-Wesley, 2000 Updated Edition.

[She 98] A. Sheer, "ARIS-Business Process Modeling" Springer-Verlag, Berlin, 1998.

[SMcD 01] A. Sharp, P. Mc Dermott, "Workflow Modeling – Tools for Process Improvement and Application Development", Artech House Publishers, 2001

[Spa 01] G. Sparks, "An Introduction to UML: The Dynamic Model", Enterprise Architect, 2001.

JOURNALS

[ATJU 95] A. Tsalgatidou and S. Junginger, "Modeling in the Re-engineering Process", ACM SIGOIS Bulletin, Special Issue: Business Process Reengineering, August 1995, Vol. 16, No. 1, pp. 17-24.

[Bro 02] Browning, R. Tayson, "Process Integration Using the Design Structure Matrix", Systems Engineering, 2002, Vol 5.3, pp 180-193.

[CBMBCF 02] C. Badica, M. Brezovan, C. Fox, "Business Process Modelling in INSPIRE Using Petri Nets", Periodica Politechnica, Transactions on Automatic Control and Computer Science, Vol. 47 (61), 2002, ISSN 1224-600X.

[DGAT 98] D. Georgakopoulos and A. Tsalgatidou, "Technology and Tools for Comprehensive Business Process Lifecycle Management", in 'Workflow Management Systems and Interoperability', Asuman Dogac, Leonid Kalinichenko, Tamer Ozsu and Amit Sheth (Eds.), NATO ASI Series F, Springer Verlag, 1998.

[ESBAPJEPBW 02] E. Söderström, B. Andersson, P. Johannesson, E. Perjons, B. Wangler, "Towards a Framework for Comparing Process Modelling Languages", A. Banks Pidduck et al. (Eds.): CAISE 2002, LNCS 2348, pp. 600-611, Springer-Verlag, Berlin, Heidelberg, 2002

[Gia 01] M. Giaglis, "A Taxonomy of Business Process Modeling and Information Systems Modelling Techniques", International Journal of Flexible Manufacturing Systems, 2001, 13(2), pp209.

[HSTJPO 02] H. Stahl, T. Jankko, P. Olttinen, "Modelling of publishing processing with UML", Journal of Graphic Arts, Finland, Vol 31,No 3, 2002, pp 10-21

[JDR 00] J. Dorador, R. Young. "Application of IDEF0, IDEF3 and UML Methodologies in the Creation of Information Models", International Journal of Computer Integrated Manufacturing, 2000,Vol.13, No 5, pp 430-445.

[JEJ 95] I. Jacobson, M. Ericsson, A. Jacobson, "The Object Advantage: Business Process Engineering with Object Technology", ACM Press, 1995.

[Kor 94] P. Korzeniowski, "Workflow Software Automates Processes", Software Magazine, 1994.

[McC92] S. McCready, “There is more than one kind of Workflow Software”, Computerworld, 1992

[MNTFVZ 98] Nüttgens, M.; Feld, T.; Zimmermann, V. “Business Process Modeling with EPC and UML: Transformation or Integration?”, In M. Schader, & A. Korthaus (Eds.). The Unified Modeling Language - Technical Aspects and Applications. Heidelberg: Springer, 1998, pp. 250-261.

[PLTA 98] P. Loos, T. Allweyer, “Process Orientation and Object-Orientation — An Approach for Integrating UML and Event-Driven Process Chains (EPC)”, Publication of the Institut für Wirtschaftsinformatik University of Saarland, Saarbrücken, Paper 144, 1998.

[THMO 95]T. Huckvale, M. Ould, “Process Modeling – Who, What and How: Role Activity Diagramming”, In: Business Process Change: Concepts, Methods and Technologies, Idea Group Publishing, 1995.

[Tsa 99] A. Tsalgatidou, "Re-engineering and Automation of Business Processes: Criteria for Selecting Supporting Tools", in 'Current Trends in Database Technology', A. Dogac, M. Tamer Ozsu and Ozgur Ulusoy (eds.), IDEA Group Publishing, 1999.

[VVCBVH 03] V. Bosilj Vuksic, C. Badica, V. Hlupic, "Petri nets and IDEF diagrams: Applicability and efficacy for business process modelling", Journal of Informatica, Vol. 25, No. 1, April 2001, pp 123-133

PROCEEDINGS

[LWBHAP 97] L. Whitman, B. Huff, A. Presley, “Structured Models and Dynamic Systems Analysis: The

Integration of the IDEF0/IDEF3 Modeling Methods and Discrete Event Simulation", ACM In the Proceedings of the 1997 Winter Simulation Conference, S. Andradottir, K. J. Healy, D. H. Withers, B. L. Nelson (eds.), 1997.

INTERNET SOURCES – WHITE PAPERS

[Fer 01] Ferdian, "A Comparison of Event-driven Process Chains and UML Activity Diagram for Denoting Business Processes", Master Thesis, Supervisor Professor: Dr. J Schmidt, Technological University of Hamburg, Information and Communication Systems, 2001

[HMGJELGTAP 03] H. Mili, G. Jaoude, E. Lefebvre, G. Tremblay,A. Petrenko, "Business Process Modeling Languages: Sorting Through the Alphabet Soup", Technical Report, November 2003, available at: http://www.info.uqam.ca/~mili/Recherche/publications.html.

[IDEF0 93] IDEF0, Announcing the Standard for Integration Definition for Function Modeling (IDEF0), FIPS PUBS, National Institute of Standards and Technology, 1993, available at: http://www.idef.com/Downloads/pdf/Idef0.pdf

[May at al 95] R. Mayer, C. Menzer, M. Painter, P. deWitte, T. Blinn, B. Perakath, IDEF3 Process Description Capture Method Report, Knowledge Based System Inc, 1995, available at: http://www.idef.com.Downloads/pdf/Idef3_fn.pdf

[MKNDACESWK 03] M. Kamath, N. Dalal, A. Chaugule, E. Sivaraman, W. Kolarik, "A Review of Enterprise Process Modeling Techniques" Lecture Notes on Systems Design and Integration, Oklahoma State University, 2003, also available at: http://www.okstate.edu/cocim/members/eswar/Fall 2003/SYST520/SESBookChapter2.pdf.

[Nor 03] O. Noran , "Business Modeling: UML vs IDEF", Griffith University, School of Computing, 2003, also available at http://www.cit.gu.edu.au/~noran./UMLvsIDEF.pdf.

[OMG 00] OMG, Unified Modeling Language Specification: Version 1.3, March 2000, available at: http://www.omg.org.

[TAPL 98] T. Allweyer, P. Loos "Process Orientation in UML trough Integration of Event-Driven Process Chains", 1998.

[TDJM 03] T. Dufresne, J. Martin, "Process Modeling for E-Business", INFS 770 – Methods for Information Systems Engineering: Knowledge Management and E-Business, Spring 2003

[Tsa 02] A. Tsalgatidou, "Business Process Modelling", Lecture Notes, National and Kapodistrian University of Athens, Department of Informatics and Telecommunications, Athens 2002.

Made in United States
Troutdale, OR
11/03/2026

56844875R00060